CHAPTERS

FROM

SOME MEMOIRS

BY

ANNE THACKERAY RITCHIE

London
MACMILLAN AND CO.
AND NEW YORK
1894

Publishing Statement:

This important reprint was made from an old and scarce book.

Therefore, it may have defects such as missing pages, erroneous pagination, blurred pages, missing text, poor pictures, markings, marginalia and other issues beyond our control.

Because this is such an important and rare work, we believe it is best to reproduce this book regardless of its original condition.

Thank you for your understanding and enjoy this unique book!

TO

GEORGE AND ELIZABETH MURRAY SMITH

THESE CHAPTERS

(*AND HOW MANY NOT WRITTEN HERE*)

ARE DEDICATED

IN AFFECTION AND FRIENDSHIP.

The End House, Wimbledon,
11*th February* 1894.

CONTENTS

CHAPTER I

CHAPTERS

FROM SOME MEMOIRS

CHAPTER I

My father lived in good company, so that even as children we must have seen a good many poets and remarkable people, though we were not always conscious of our privileges. Things certainly strike children oddly, partially, and for unexpected reasons. They are so busy in early life with all that is going on on every side, that one person or another person, the visitor in the drawing-room, the tortoise-shell cat on the garden wall, the cook's little boy who has come in to partake of cold pudding, all seem very nearly as important one as the other. Perhaps I should not have been so much impressed by my first conscious sight of a poet, if I had then realised all the notabilities who came to our house from time to time. My special poet was a Frenchman. I first heard his name in London, at a class which I attended in company with a good many other little girls, my contemporaries—which class indeed still continues, and succeeding generations receive the decorations, the *présidences* and the *sous présidences*, I fear I personally never attained to.

My poet was a hairdresser by profession and a barber as well. His name was Jasmin (Jaquou Jansemin in the *langue d'Oc*). He was born in 1798 at Agen in the south of France; "born," he writes, "of a humpback father and a halting mother in the corner of an old street, in a crowded dwelling, peopled by many rats, on Holy Thursday, at the hour when pancakes are tossed." The humpback father was also a poet in his way, and composed songs for the itinerant players of the neighbourhood. So soon as Jasmin could walk he used to accompany his father to the booths, but what he liked better still was gathering faggots in the little islands of the Garonne. "Bare-headed, bare-footed," he writes, "we rowed across the stream. I was not alone,—there were twenty of us—there were thirty of us.

We started at the stroke of the mid-day hour, singing in choir." In the evening the children returned as they had left, — "thirty voices chaunting the same cadence, and thirty faggots dancing on thirty heads." They were so poor that Jacques felt it bitterly, because his parents could not afford to send him to school. One day he was playing in the market-place when he saw his grandfather carried by to the hospital. It was there the Jasmins were in the habit of dying. But a cousin taught him to read; he became apprenticed to a barber, he rose to be a hairdresser, and prospered in his vocation; so that he was able to save his father from the usual fate of the Jasmins.

The young hairdresser christened his first poems *Les Papillotes*, in honour of his profession; "which songs," says he, "brought a silver streamlet through my shop"; and upon this streamlet he floated to better fortunes than were usual to the Jasmin family. One day in a fit of poetic ardour he broke the terrible arm-chair in which they had all been in the habit of being carried to the hospital. Jasmin after he became celebrated would never abandon his home or his little shop,

but from time to time he went for a journey;
sometimes he would come to Paris, where he was
kindly recognised by other authors more fortunate in their worldly circumstances, and he would
be made to repeat his own songs by the great
ladies who took him up. Chief among them
was Lady Elgin, who lived in Paris then, and
who was a good friend to all literary aspirants.
Longfellow was also among Jasmin's admirers,
and translated some of his works. Much of all
this I have since read in the *Biographie
Nationale*. As children at our French class we
had only learnt some of his lines by heart. I
used to break down in utter confusion when my
turn came to recite; but at the same time I
believe I took in a great deal more than I had
any idea of, as I sat there incompetent, wool-
gathering. In that long, bare room, only
ornamented by a few large maps and with a
flowing border of governesses, there came to
one many of those impressions which are not
dates or facts, and which don't, alas! count for
good marks, but which nevertheless are very
useful and agreeable possessions in after days.
We used to have delightful French lessons in

literature and poetry, and I still remember the dazzling visions of troubadours evoked by our teacher, troubadours amid the golden land-scapes of the south of France;—the poems themselves as he quoted them almost seemed to have wings and to come flying out of the well-thumbed *Recueil!*

We had lessons in morality and in experience as well as in literature. I can still hear M. Roche in his melodious voice quoting "de tout laurier un poison est l'essence," and praising the philosophical aptness of the illustration, which seemed to me so splendid that I was quite overpowered by it as I went home with my governess along South Audley Street. There was another heart-rending poem about an angel standing by a cradle and contemplating its own image in the face of the infant, "reflected as in a stream." The angel finally carries away the poor baby, and the mother kneels weeping by the empty cradle. It was a sort of Christmas-card of a poem well suited to the sentimental experience of a little girl of twelve or thirteen years old; and I then and there determined that Reboul was my favourite author of all. But there were many others besides Reboul. Poor André Chenier we were all in love with, and Jasmin aforesaid held his own among the worthy recipients of that golden flower of poesy which played such an important part in our early education, and which was (so we learnt) yearly bestowed by the inhabitants of Toulouse upon the most successful competitors in the art. I used to picture the flower itself as a radiant quivering object covered with delicate, glittering work-manship. Perhaps nowadays I realise that golden flowers of poesy are also bestowed in the south of England,—in Waterloo Place, or Bedford Street, Covent Garden, shall we say ? —round golden tokens which are not without their own special graces.

But to return to my memoirs. Our life was divided between London and Paris, where our grandparents dwelt, and where we spent a part of every year ; and all my recent studies and experiences rushed into my mind one day, soon after our return to France, when my grand-mother told me that she had been asked to a party at Lady Elgin's to meet a poet, that his

name was Jasmin, and that she was going to
take me with her! My heart leapt with excitement; Jasmin—the South—golden flowers—
présidences—a grown-up party—the portals of
life seemed to fly open with those of our *porte-
cochère* as the carriage, containing my grandmother and me in our Sunday best, drove off
into the dark streets. We were escorted downstairs by the cook, with an extra lantern, I remember, and my grandfather in his little black
silk toque waved farewell over the staircase.
We started expectant, rolling over the rattling
stones; we crossed the bridge and saw the
dark river below us reflecting the lights—I
remember no stars, but a damp and drizzly
darkness overhead, which for some reason
added to my excitement. We reached the
ancient faubourg before very long, where the
oil-lamps swung by chains across the streets;
we turned into the Rue de Varennes where
Lady Elgin lived, and the coachman rapped at
the great closed gates of the house, which
opened with a grinding sound, and we walked
across the courtyard. The apartment was on
the ground-floor of a fine melancholy old house.

I followed my grandmother in her brown velvet gown and her diamond brooch into the reception-room. I remember being surprised to find the gay world so dark on the whole, and talking in such a confused and subdued murmur. I had expected chandeliers, bursts of laughter, people in masks and dominoes. I had taken my ideas from bonbon boxes and crackers. But it was evidently all right, my grandmother looked greatly pleased and animated. I saw her speaking to one person and to another in her dignified way—her manners were true grandmother's manners, kind, but distant and serious. We considered our grandmother a very important personage, and I remember feeling not a little proud of her beauty and dignity as we moved along. She was not one of your "remains"; she was a very noble-looking old lady, holding her head high, and her diamond cap-pin flashed as she moved across the room.

My grandmother, as I have said, looked pleased and animated, and when her friends came up to speak to her she introduced me to some of them. Almost the very first person she greeted, but to whom she did not introduce me, was a handsome, rather romantic, fashionable-looking gentleman, with a quantity of dark hair, and a glass in one eye, leaning against the wall by the door as we entered. She said a few words as we passed; I heard something about "Lady Charlotte," and then we walked on, and presently we came upon another girl, younger than myself and very distinguished-looking, in a plaid frock, with beautiful shining braids of thick hair, who seemed quite at home and used to the house; she was with her mother, a regal-looking little woman with a profile and a gold crown; I can still see her in a long green velvet robe slowly crossing the room; she was a well-known person, Mrs. Chapman, the celebrated Abolitionist; the little girl was her youngest daughter. While Mrs. Chapman and my grandmother were talking to one another, little Anne Chapman, who seemed to know most of the people, began telling me who they all were. A great many pages out of M. Roche's *Recueil* were present. There were all sorts of notable folks murmuring to one another in the big rooms. "Who was the gentleman in the doorway?" "Oh, he is Mr. Locker," said little Anne, "he is married to Lady Charlotte— Lady Elgin's daughter; didn't I know?—they had only come over from England the day before." "And which is the poet?" said I eagerly. "There he is, in the middle of the room," said the little girl. "Oh, where?" said I. "Oh, not *that!*" For suddenly, just under the swinging chandelier, I see a head, like the figure-head of a ship—a jolly, red, shiny, weather-beaten face, with large round prominent features, ornamented with little pomatumy wisps of hair, and a massive torso clothed in a magnificent frilled shirt over a pink lining. . . "*That* the poet? not that," I falter, gazing at Punchinello, high-shouldered, good-humoured! "Yes, of course it is that," said the little girl, laughing at my dismay; and the crowd seems to form a circle, in the centre of which stands this droll being, who now begins to recite in a monotonous voice.

I can understand French well enough, but not one single word of what he is saying. It sounds perfectly unintelligible, something like *chi, chou, cha, atchiou, atchiou, atchiou!* And

so it goes on, and on, and on. The shirt frill
beats time, the monotonous voice rises and
falls. It leaves off at last, the poet wipes the
perspiration from his brow ; there is a moment's
silence, then a murmur of admiration from the
crowd which closes round him. I see the
Punchinello being led up to somebody to be
thanked and congratulated ; my heart goes
down, down ; more murmurs, more exclamations. The little girl is gone, I am all alone
with my disappointment, and then my grandmother calls me to her side and says it is time
to come away. As we move towards the door
again, we once more pass Mr. Locker, and he
nods kindly, and tells me he knows my father.
"Well, and what do you think of Jasmin ?" he
asks ; but I can't answer him, my illusions are
dashed.

As we drive off through the streets the rain
is still falling, the oil-lamps are swinging ; we
cross the bridge once more, but how dull, how
dark, how sad it all seems ! My grandmother,
sitting upright in the dark carriage, says she
has spent a very pleasant evening, and that
she is delighted with Jasmin's simplicity and

originality. I who had longed to see a poet! who had pictured something so different! I swallowed down as best I could that gulp of salt water which is so apt to choke us when we first take our plunge into the experience of life. "He didn't *look* much like a poet, and I couldn't understand what he said," I faltered.

"Of course you could not understand the *patois*, but have you not enjoyed your evening?" said my grandmother, disappointed. I had the grace to try to speak cheerfully. "I liked the little girl very much, and—and—and I liked talking to Mr. Locker, but then he *isn't* a poet," said I.

I can't help laughing even now as I conjure up the absurd little dream of the past and the bitterness of that childish disappointment. How little do we mortals recognise our good fortune that comes to us now and again in a certain humorous disguise. Why, I had been in a world of poets! A poet had greeted me, a poet had sung to me, I had been hustled by poets; there in the crowd (for all I know to the contrary) were Lamartine and Chateaubriand and Girardin and Mérimée,—so at least some one who was present on this occasion reminds me. And as for Frederick Locker, does not his caged music—like that of the bird of Wood Street—echo along the arid pavements with sweetest and most welcome note to charm the passers-by as the echoes of _London Lyrics_ fall upon the listening ear? And the red face was also that of a true poet, born to sing his sweet unpretending song from a true heart, and to bring music into humble places. "A poet of the people, writing in his dialect, celebrating public occasions and solemnities," says Sainte-Beuve, "which somehow remind one of the Middle Ages; belonging" (so he continues) "to the school of Horace and to the school of Theocritus and to that of Gray, and to that of all those charming studious inspirations which aim at perfection in all their work."

CHAPTER II

MY MUSICIAN

ONE's early life is certainly a great deal more amusing to look back to than it used to be when it was going on. For one thing, it isn't nearly so long now as it was then, and remembered events come cheerfully scurrying up one after another, while the intervening periods are no longer the portentous cycles they once used to be. And another thing to consider is that the people walking in and out of the bygone mansions of life were not, to our newly-opened eyes, the interesting personages many of them have since become; *then* they were men walking as trees before us, without names or histories,—*now* some of the very names mean for us the history of our time. Very young people's eyes are certainly of more importance to them than their ears, and they all *see* the persons they are destined to spend their lives with long before the figures begin to talk and to explain themselves.

My grandmother had a little society of her own at Paris, in the midst of which she seemed to reign from dignity and kindness of heart; her friends, it must be confessed, have not as yet become historic, but she herself was well worthy of a record. Grandmothers in books and memoirs are mostly alike, stately, old-fashioned, kindly, and critical. Mine was no exception to the general rule. She had been one of the most beautiful women of her time; she was very tall, with a queenly head and carriage; she always moved in a dignified way. She had an odd taste in dress, I remember, and used to walk out in a red merino cloak trimmed with ermine, which gave her the air of a retired empress wearing out her robes. She was a woman of strong feeling, somewhat imperious, with a passionate love for little children, and with extraordinary sympathy and enthusiasm for any one in trouble or in disgrace. How benevolently she used to look round the room at her many *protégés*, with her beautiful gray eyes! Her friends as a rule were shorter than she was and brisker, less serious and emotional. They adopted her views upon politics, religion and homœopathy, or at all events did not venture to contradict them. But they certainly could not reach her heights, and her almost romantic passion of feeling.

A great many of my earliest recollections seem to consist of old ladies,—regiments of old ladies, so they appear to me, as I look back through the larger end of my glasses to the time when my sister and I were two little girls living at Paris. I remember once that after a long stay in England with our father, the old ladies seemed changed somehow to our more experienced eyes. They were the same, but with more variety; not all alike as they had seemed before, not all the same age; some were younger, some were older than we had remembered them—one was actually married! Our grandmother looked older to us this time when we came back to Paris. We were used to seeing our father's gray hair, but that hers should turn white too seemed almost unnatural.

The very first day we walked out with her after our return, we met the bride of whose marriage we had heard while we were away. She was a little, dumpy, good-natured woman of about forty-five, I suppose,—shall I ever forget the thrill with which we watched her approach, hanging with careless grace upon her husband's arm? She wore light, tight kid gloves upon her little fat hands, and a bonnet like a bride's-cake. Marriage had not made her proud as it does some people; she recognised us at once and introduced us to the gentleman. "Very 'appy to make your acquaintance, miss," said he. "Mrs. C. 'ave often mentioned you at our place."

Children begin by being Philistines. As we parted I said to my grandmother that I had always known people dropped their h's, but that I didn't know one ever married them. My grandmother seemed trying not to laugh, but she answered gravely that Mr. and Mrs. C. looked very happy, h's or no h's. And so they did, walking off along those illuminated Elysian fields gay with the echoes of Paris in May, while the children capered to itinerant music,

and flags were flying and penny trumpets ringing, and strollers and spectators were lining the
way, and the long interminable procession of
carriages in the centre of the road went rolling
steadily towards the Bois de Boulogne. As we
walked homewards evening after evening the
sun used to set splendidly in the very centre of
the great triumphal arch at the far end of the
avenue, and flood everything in a glorious tide
of light.   What, indeed, did an aspirate more or
less matter at such a moment!

I don't think we ever came home from one
of our walks that we did not find our grandfather sitting watching for our grandmother's
return. We used to ask him if he didn't find
it very dull doing nothing in the twilight, but
he used to tell us it was his thinking-time. My
sister and I thought thinking dreadfully dull,
and only longed for candles and *Chambers's
Miscellany*. A good deal of thinking went on
in our peaceful home, we should have liked more
doing. One day was just like another; my
grandmother and my grandfather sat on either
side of the hearth in their two accustomed
places ; there was a French cook in a white cap,

who brought in the trays and the lamp at the appointed hour; there was Chambers on the book-shelf, *Pickwick*, and one or two of my father's early books, and *The Listener*, by Caroline Fry, which used to be my last desperate resource when I had just finished all the others. We lived in a sunny little flat on a fourth floor, with windows east and west and a wide horizon from each, and the sound of the cries from the street below, and the confusing roll of the wheels when the windows were open in summer. In winter time we dined at five by lamplight at the round table in my grandfather's study. After dinner we used to go into the pretty blue drawing-room, where the peat fire would be burning brightly in the open grate, and the evening paper would come in with the tea. I can see it all still, hear it, smell the peat, and taste the odd herbaceous tea and the French bread and butter. On the band of the *Constitutional* newspaper was printed " M. le Major Michel Eschmid." It was not my grandfather's name or anything like it, but he would gravely say that when English people lived in France they must expect to have their names gallicised, and his paper certainly found him out evening. after evening. While my grandmother with much emphasis read the news (she was a fervent republican, and so was my grandfather), my sister and I would sit unconscious of politics and happy over our story-books, until the fatal inevitable moment when a ring was heard at the bell and evening callers were announced. Then we reluctantly shut up our books, for we were told to get our needlework when the company came in, and we had to find chairs and hand tea-cups, and answer inquiries, and presently go to bed.

The ladies would come in in their bonnets, with their news and their comments upon the public events, which, by the way, seemed to go off like fireworks in those days expressly for our edification. Ours was a talkative, economical, and active little society,—*Cranford en Voyage* is the impression which remains to me of those early surroundings. If the ladies were one and all cordially attached to my grandmother, to my grandfather they were still more devoted. A Major is a Major. He used to sign their pension papers, administer globules for their colds, give point and support to their political opinions.   I can see him still sitting in his arm-chair by the fire with a little semicircle round about the hearth.   Ours was anything but a meek and disappointed community.   We may have had our reverses,—and very important reverses they all seem to have been,—but we had all had spirit enough to leave our native shores and settle in Paris, not without a certain implied disapproval of the other people who went on living in England regardless of expense. My father did not escape this criticism.   Why, they used to say, did he remain in that nasty smoky climate, so bad for health and spirits? Why didn't he settle in Paris and write works upon the French?   Why didn't I write and coax him to come, and tell him that it was our grandmother's wish that he should do so, that the speaker, Mademoiselle Trotkins (or who-ever it might be), had told me to write?   I remember going through an early martyrdom at these friendly hands, and bitterly and silently resenting their indignation with any one who could prefer that black and sooty place London to Paris.   At the same time they allowed that

the *loyers* were becoming more exorbitant every
day, and as for the *fruitière* at the corner she
was charging no less than forty *sous* for her
Isyngny.   We always talked in a sort of sand-
wich of French and English.   Oddly enough,
though we talked French, and some of us even
looked French, we knew no French people.
From time to time at other houses I used to
hear of real foreigners, but I don't remember
seeing any at ours, except a *pasteur* who sometimes came, and a certain Vicomte de B. (I had
nearly written Bragelonne), whose mother, I
believe, was also English.   *Jeunes filles, jeunes
fleurs*, he used to say, bowing to the younger
ladies.   This was our one only approach to an
introduction to French society.   But all the
same, one cannot live abroad without imbibing
something of the country, of the air and the
earth and the waters among which one is living.
Breath and food and raiment are a part of one's
life, after all, and a very considerable part ; and
all the wonderful tide of foreign sunshine and
the cheerful crowds and happy voices outside,
and the very click of pots and pans in the little
kitchen at the back seemed to have a character

of their own. And so, though we knew nothing of the French, we got to know France and to feel at home there beneath its blue sky ; and I think to this day a holiday abroad is ten times more a holiday than a holiday at home. From mere habit one seems to be sixteen again, and one's spirits rise and one's exigencies abate. Besides the dwellers in the *appartements* and the regular customers of the extortionate *fruitière*, there used to be passing friends and acquaintances who visited us on their way to other resorts—to Italy, to the German baths. Some stopped in Paris for a week or two at a time, others for a few days only.

I remember three Scotch ladies, for whom my grandmother had a great regard, who were not part of our community, but who used to pass through Paris, and always made a certain stay. . . . I was very much afraid of them, though interested at the same time as girls are in unknown quantities. They were well connected and had estates and grand relations in the distance, though they seemed to live as simply as we did. One winter it was announced that they had taken an apartment for a few weeks, and next morning I was sent with a note to one of them by my grandmother. They were tall, thin ladies, two were widows, one was a spinster; of the three the unmarried one frightened me most. On this occasion, after reading the note, one of the widow ladies said to the spinster Miss X., who had her bonnet on, "Why, you were just going to call on the child's grandmother, were you not? Why don't you take her back with you in the carriage?" "I must first go and see how he is this morning," said Miss X., somewhat anxiously, "and then I will take her home, of course. Are the things packed?" A servant came in carrying a large basket with a variety of bottles and viands and napkins. I had not presence of mind to run away as I longed to do, and somehow in a few minutes I found myself sitting in a little open carriage with the Scotch lady, and the basket on the opposite seat. I thought her, if possible, more terrible than ever—she seemed grave, preoccupied. She had a long nose, a thick brown complexion, grayish sandy hair, and was dressed in scanty cloth skirts, gray and sandy too. She spoke to

me, I believe, but my heart was in my mouth ;
I hardly dared even listen to what she said.
We drove along the Champs Elysées towards
the Arc, and then turned into a side street, and
presently came to a house at the door of which
the carriage stopped. The lady got out, carefully carrying her heavy basket, and told me to
follow, and we began to climb the shiny stairs
—one, two flights I think ; then we rang at a
bell and the door was almost instantly opened.
It was opened by a slight, delicate-looking man
with long hair, bright eyes, and a thin, hooked
nose. When Miss X. saw him she hastily put
down her basket upon the floor, caught both
his hands in hers, began to shake them gently,
and to scold him in an affectionate reproving
way for having come to the door. He laughed,
said he had guessed who it was, and motioned
to her to enter, and I followed at her sign with
the basket,—followed into a narrow little room,
with no furniture in it whatever but an upright
piano against the wall and a few straw chairs
standing on the wooden shiny floor. He made
us sit down with some courtesy, and in reply to
her questions said he was pretty well. Had he

hurriedly said we must go; but as we took leave she added almost in a whisper with a humble apologising look,—" I have brought you some of that jelly, and my sister sent some of the wine you fancied the other day; pray, pray, try to take a little." He again shook his head at her, seeming more vexed than grateful. " It is very wrong; you shouldn't bring me these things," he said in French. " I won't play to you if you do,"—but she put him back softly, and hurriedly closed the door upon him and the offending basket, and hastened away. As we were coming downstairs she wiped her eyes again. By this time I had got to understand the plain, tall, grim, warm-hearted woman; all my silly terrors were gone. She looked hard at me as we drove away. " Never forget that you have heard Chopin play," she said with emotion, " for soon no one will ever hear him play any more."

Sometimes reading the memoirs of the great musician, the sad story of his early death, of his passionate fidelity, and cruel estrangement from the companion he most loved, I have remembered this little scene with comfort and pleasure, and known that he was not altogether alone in life, and that he had good friends who cared for his genius and tended him to the last. Of their affection he was aware. But of their constant secret material guardianship he was unconscious; the basket he evidently hated, the woman he turned to with most grateful response and dependence. He was to the very end absorbed in his music, in his art, in his love. He had bestowed without counting all that he had to give: he poured it forth upon others, never reckoning the cost: and then dying away from it all, he in turn took what came to him as a child might do, without pondering or speculating overmuch.

CHAPTER III

MY TRIUMPHAL ARCH

I BEGAN life at four or five years old as a fervent Napoleonist. The great Emperor had not been dead a quarter of a century when I was a little child. He was certainly alive in the hearts of the French people and of the children growing up among them. Influenced by the cook we adored his memory, and the *concierge* had a clock with a laurel wreath which for some reason kindled all our enthusiasm.

As a baby holding my father's finger I had stared at the second funeral of Napoleon sweeping up the great roadway of the Champs Elysées. The ground was white with new-fallen snow, and I had never seen snow before; it seemed to me to be a part of the funeral; a mighty pall indeed, spread for the obsequies of

so great a warrior.   It was the snow I thought
about, though I looked with awe at the black
and glittering carriages which came up like
ships sailing past us, noiselessly one by one.
They frightened me, for I thought there was a
dead emperor in each.   This weird procession
gave a strange importance to the memory of
the great Emperor, and also to the little marble
statuette of him on the nursery chimney-piece.
It stood with folded arms contemplating the
decadence of France, black and silent and
reproachful.   France was no longer an empire,
only a kingdom just like any other country ; this
fact I and the cook bitterly resented.   Besides
the statuette there was a snuff-box, belonging I
know not to whom, that was a treasure of
emotional awe.   It came out on Sundays, and
sometimes of an evening just before bed-time.
At first as you looked you saw nothing but the
cover of a wooden box ornamented by a drawing
in brown sepia, the sketch of a tomb-stone and
a weeping willow-tree,—nothing more.   Then
if you looked again, indicated by ingenious
twigs and lines there gradually dawned upon
you the figure, the shadowy figure of him who

lay beneath the stone. Napoleon, pale and
sad, with folded arms, with his cocked hat
crushed forward on his brow, the mournful
shade of the conqueror who had sent a million
of other men to Hades before him.

As we gazed we hated the English. It is
true, I was very glad they always conquered
everybody, and that my grandpapa was a major
in their army ; but at the same time the cook
and I hated the perfidious English, and we felt
that if Napoleon had not been betrayed he
would still have been reigning over us here in
Paris.

Every day we children used to go with our
bonne to play round about the Arc de Triomphe,
near which we lived, and where, alternating
with ornamental rosettes, the long lists of
Napoleon's battles and triumphs were carved
upon the stone. The *bonne* sat at work upon
one of the stone benches which surround the
Arc, we made gravel pies on the step at her
feet and searched for shells in the sand, or when
we were not prevented by the guardian, swung
on the iron chains which divide the inclosure
from the road. We paid no attention whatever

to the inscriptions, in fact we couldn't read very
well in those days. We hardly ever looked at
the groups of statuary, except that there was
one great arm carrying a shield, and a huge leg
like the limb in the Castle of Otranto which
haunted us, and which we always saw, though
we tried *not* to see it.   I never remember being
very light-hearted or laughing at my play up
by the Arc, a general sense of something grim
and great and strange and beyond my small
ken impressed itself upon me as we played.
When I had nightmares at night, the Arc de
Triomphe, with its writhing figures, was always
mixed up with them.   One day the guardian
in his brass buttons, being in a good humour,
allowed us all to climb up without paying, to
the flat lead terrace on the top.   There were
easy steps inside the walls, and slits for light
at intervals ; and when we climbed up the last
steep step and came out upon the summit we
saw the great view, the domes and the pinnacles
and gilt weathercocks of the lovely city all
spreading before us, and the winding river, and
the people looking like grains of sand blown by
the wind, and the carriages crawling like insects,

and the palace of the Tuileries in its lovely old gardens shining with its pinnacles. But somehow the world from a monumental height is quite different from what it seems from a curbstone, where much more human impressions are to be found; and that disembodied Paris, spreading like a vision, never appeared to me to be the same place as the noisy, cheerful, beloved city of my early childish recollections.

The first house in which we lived at Paris was an old house in an old avenue enclosed by iron gates which were shut at night. It was called the Avenue Sainte-Marie, and led from the Faubourg du Roule to the Arc de Triomphe. The avenue was planted with shady trees; on one side of it there were houses, on the other convent walls. At the door of one of the houses an old man sat in his chair, who used to tell us as we passed by that in a few months he would be a hundred years old, and then they would put him into the papers. I used to play in the courtyard belonging to the house in which we lived. There was a pump, and there was a wall with a row of poplar trees beyond it. There was a faded fresco painted on the wall, a dim fountain, a pale Italian garden, a washed-out bird flying away with a blue tail across long streaks of mildew that had come from the drippings of the trees. Frescoes must have been in fashion at the time when the Avenue Sainte-Marie was built, for there was also a dim painting on the convent wall opposite our porte cochère, representing a temple in a garden and clouds, and another bird with outstretched wings. From beyond this wall we used to hear the bells and the litanies of the nuns. One night I dreamt that I was walking in the convent garden, and that my father came out of the temple to fetch me home, and that the bird flapped its wings with a shrill cry. I used to dream a great deal when I was a little child, and then wake up in my creaking wooden bed, and stare at the dim floating night-light like a little ship on its sea of oil. Then from the dark corners of the room there used to come all sorts of strange things sailing up upon the darkness. I could see them all looking like painted pictures. There were flowers, birds, dolls, toys, shining things of every description.

I have since heard that this seeing of pictures in the dark is not an uncommon faculty among children. My chief playmate in those days was the concierge's niece, who used to go to school at the convent. She used to wear a black stuff pinafore and a blue riband with the image of the Virgin round her neck. As we played we could hear other music than that of the nuns, the brilliant strains of Monsieur Ernest's piano in the apartment over ours. He was a kind young man, very fond of children, who used to open the window and play to us brilliant dances and marches which we delighted in; when he ceased we went back to our games.

It was later in life that with the help, either of Justine or another relation of the family, I tried to polish up the stairs as a surprise for the porter on his return from an errand. We got the long brooms and sticks out of the lodge, where there was nobody to be seen, only an odd smell and a great pot simmering by the fire. One of us carried a feather broom, the other a brush with a strap to it and a great stick with a bit of wax at one end. Then we set to work, not forgetting the hissing sound.

Justine flapped about with the feather broom and duster; I tried to work my foot with the heavy brush, but the brush flies off, the broom clatters echoing down the stairs, the waxed stick falls over the banisters, some one screams, doors open, voices are heard; I have thumped my nose, bumped my forehead, but I do not mind the pain, the disgrace and ignominy of failure are far more terrible.

I cannot clearly remember when I became an Orleanist, but I think I must have been about six years old at the time, standing tip-toe on the aforesaid curb-stone.   My grandmother had changed her cook and her apartment, and I had happened to hear my grandfather say that Napoleon was a rascal who had *not* been betrayed by the English.   Then came a day—shall I ever forget it ?—when a yellow carriage jingled by with a beautiful little smiling boy at the window, a fair-haired, blue-eyed prince.   It was the little Comte de Paris, who would be a king some day they told me, and who was smiling and looking so charming that then and there I deserted my colours and went over to the camp of the Orleans.   Alas! that the lilies of France should have been smirched and soiled by base and vulgar intrigues, and that my little prince should have stepped down unabashed, as a gray-headed veteran, from the dignified shrine of his youth. I remember once hearing my father say of the Duc d'Aumale, "He has everything in his favour, good looks, dignity, fine manners, intellect, riches, and above all misfortune"; and with all of these I invested the image of my own particular little prince.

One *mi-carême*, on that mysterious pagan feast of the butchers, when the fat ox, covered with garlands and with gilded horns, is led to sacrifice through the streets of Paris, I also to my great satisfaction was brought forth to join the procession by a couple of maids, one of whom carried a basket. I remember finding my stumpy self in a court of the Tuileries, the fairy ox having been brought thither for the benefit of the King, and I was hustled to the front of a crowd and stood between my two protectors looking up at a window. Then comes an outcry of cheering, and a venerable, curly-headed old gentleman, Louis Philippe himself, just like all his pictures, appears for an

instant behind the glass, and then the people
shout again and again, and the window opens
and the King steps out on to the balcony
handing out an old lady in a bonnet and frizzed
white curls, and, yes, the little boy is there too.
Hurrah, hurrah! for all the kings and queens!
And somebody is squeezing me up against the
basket, but I am now an Orleanist and ready
to suffer tortures for the kind old grandpapa
and the little boy. Now that I am a gray-
headed woman I feel as if I could still stand
in the crowd and cry hurrah! for honest men
who, with old Louis Philippe, would rather
give up their crowns than let their subjects
be fired upon ; and if my little prince, instead
of shabbily intriguing with adventurers, had
kept to his grandfather's peaceful philosophy
I could have cried hurrah! for him still with
all my heart.

I suppose we have most of us, in and out of
our pinafores, stood by triumphal archways put
up for other people, and moralised a little bit
before proceeding to amuse ourselves with our
own adventures further on. As I have said,
the Arc de Triomphe seems mixed up with all

my early life. I remember looking up at it on
my way to my first school in an adjoining street,
crossing the open space, and instead of stopping
to pick up shells as usual, casting, I daresay,
a complaisant glance of superiority at the gods
of war in their stony chariots, who, after all,
never had much education. I was nicely dressed
in a plaid frock, and wore two tails of hair tied
with ribbons, a black apron, and two little black
pantalettes. It was the admired costume of all
the young ladies of the school to which I was
bound. On this occasion the stony gods
witnessed my undue elation and subsequent
discomfiture unmoved. The triumphal arch
was certainly not intended for my return ; I was
led home that evening, after a day mostly spent
in the corner, crestfallen and crushed by my
inferiority to all the other young ladies of the
school in their black pinafores and pantalettes.

But the images round about the Arc are not
all of discomfitures and funerals and terrible
things. There were also merry-makings to be
remembered. Did not the Siamese Twins
themselves set up their booths in its shadow
in company with various wild Bedouins their

companions? I thought it cruel of the nurse
not to take me in to see the show ; and indeed
on one occasion I ran away from home to visit
it on my own account. The expedition was not
a success, but Siam has always seemed to me an
interesting country ever since. Besides the
Twins and their booth there were cafés and
resting-places in those days all round about the
Arc, and people enjoying themselves after their
day's work with song and laughter. Wild
flowers were still growing at the upper end of
the Champs Elysées on a green mound called
the Pelouse.

In the year '48, when we walked out with
our grandparents, the Pelouse had been dug
up and levelled, I think to give work to the
starving people. It was a year of catastrophes
and revolutions—a sort of "General Post"
among Kings and Governments. Many of
the promenaders (my grandparents among
them) used to wear little tricolour rosettes to
show their sympathies with the Republic.
Shall I ever forget the sight of the enthusiastic
crowds lining the way to see the President
entering Paris in a cocked hat on a curveting

Arabian steed at the head of his troops? to
be followed in a year or two by the still more
splendid apparition of Napoleon III. riding
into Paris along the road the great Emperor's
hearse had taken—a new Emperor, glittering
and alive once more, on a horse so beautiful
and majestic that to look upon it was a martial
education!

The pomp and circumstance of war were
awakened again, and troops came marching up
the avenues as before, and then, what is even
more vivid to my mind, a charming Empress
presently rose before us, winning all hearts by
her grace and her beautiful *toilettes.*   My sister
and I stood by the roadside on her wedding
day and watched her carriage rolling past the
Arc to St. Cloud; the morning had been full
of spring sunshine, but the afternoon was bleak
and drear, and I remember how we shivered
as we stood.   Some years later, when we were
no longer little girls but young ladies in crinolines, we counted the guns fired for the birth of
the Prince Imperial at the Tuileries.

CHAPTER IV

MY PROFESSOR OF HISTORY

OUR father was away in America, and we were living once more with our grandparents. We were children no longer, but young ladies supposed to be finishing our education. It will be seen that it was of a fitful and backward description. Macaulay's *Essays, Ivanhoe* and the *Talisman,* Herodotus, Milman's *History of the Jews,* and one or two stray scraps of poetry, represented our historical studies. Then came a vast and hopeless chaos in our minds reaching as far back as the times of Charlemagne and Clovis, and Bertha with the long foot, and Fredegonde who was always plunging her dagger into somebody's back. The early Merovingians will for me ever be associated with a faint smell of snuff and a plaid linen

pocket-handkerchief carefully folded; with a
little, old, short, stumpy figure, in a black cap
and dressed in a scanty black skirt. The figure
is that of my Professor of History. An old,
old lady, very short, very dignified, uttering
little grunts at intervals, and holding a pair of
spectacles in one hand and a little old black fat
book in the other, from which, with many
fumblings and snuff-takings, the good soul
would proceed to read to us of murder,
battle, rapine, and sudden death, of kings,
crowns, dynasties, and knights in armour,
while we her pupils listened, trying not to
laugh when she turned two pages at once,
or read the same page twice over with great
seriousness.

My dear grandmother, who was always in-
venting ways of helping people, and who firmly
believed in all her *protégés*, having visited our
Madame once or twice and found her absorbed
in the said history book, had arranged that a
series of historical lectures, with five-franc
tickets of admission to the course, should be
given by her during the winter months; and
that after the lecture, which used to take place

in our sitting-room, and was attended by a certain number of ladies, we should all adjourn for tea to the blue drawing-room, where the Major meanwhile had been able to enjoy his after-dinner nap in quiet. He refused to attend the course, saying, after the first lecture, that he found it difficult to follow the drift of Madame's arguments. There used to be a class of four girls, my sister and myself, our cousin Amy and Laura C., a friend of my own age—and then the occasional ladies, in bonnets, from up-stairs and downstairs and next door. The lecture lasted an hour by the clock; then the meeting suddenly adjourned, and by the time the golden flower-vase pendule in the drawing-room struck ten everybody was already walking down the shiny staircase and starting for home. Paris streets at night may be dark and muddy, or freezing cold, but they never give one that chill, vault-like feeling which London streets are apt to produce when one turns out from a warm fireside into the raw night. The ladies thought nothing of crossing the road and walking along a boulevard till they reached their own doors. Good old Madame used to walk off with those of her pupils who lived her way; they generally left her at the bright chemist's shop round the corner, where Madame Marton, the chemist's wife, would administer an evening dose of peppermint-water to keep out the cold—so we used to be told by Madame. The old lady lived in one of the tall, shabby houses at the top of the Faubourg, just behind the Arc. We used to find her sitting in a small crowded room, with a tiny ante-room, and an alcove for her bed. There she lived with her poodle, Bibi, among the faded treasures and ancient snuff-boxes and books and portraits and silhouettes of a lifetime; grim effigies of a grim past, somewhat softened by dust and time. In the midst of all the chaos one lovely miniature used to hang, shining like a star through the clouds of present loneliness and the spiders' webs of age and poverty. This was the portrait of the beautiful Lady Almeria Carpenter, the friend of Sir Joshua, with whom in some mysterious romantic way Madame was connected. Another equally valued relic was a needlebook which had been used by the Duchesse de Praslin on the day when her husband murdered her.

Madame's sister had been governess there for many years, and had loved the Duchess dearly and been valued by her, and many and mysterious were the confidences poured into my grandmother's ear concerning this sad tragedy. Our cheery, emphatic, mysterious old lady was very popular among us all. One of her kindest friends was my father's cousin, Miss R., who had lived in Paris all her life, and whose visiting-list comprised any one in trouble or poor or lonely and afflicted. I think if it had not been for her help and that of my grandmother our good old friend would have often gone through sore trials. When my father himself came to Paris to fetch us away, he was interested in the accounts he heard of the old lady from his mother and cousin. And Madame is the heroine of a little story which I have seen in print somewhere, and which I know to be true; for was I not sent one day to search for a certain pill-box in my father's room, of which he proceeded to empty the contents into the fireplace, and then drawing a neat banker's roll from his pocket, he filled up the little cube with a certain number of new napoleons; packing them in

closely up to the brim.   After which, the cover
being restored, he wrote the following prescrip-
tion in his beautiful even handwriting : *Madame
P . . . . To be taken occasionally when required.
Signed Dr. W. M. T.*"   Which medicine my
grandmother, greatly pleased, promised to administer to her old friend after our departure.

The remembrance of this pill-box and of my
father's kind hands packing up the napoleons
came to me long after, at a time when mis-
fortunes of every kind had fallen upon the
familiar friends and places of our early youth,
when the glare of burning Paris seemed to
reach us far away in our English homes, and
we almost thought we could hear the thunders
breaking on the unhappy city.   We thought of
our poor old lady, alone with her dear Bibi, in
the midst of all this terror and destruction.   As
we sat down to our legs of mutton we pictured
the horrible *salmis* and *fricandeaus* of rats and
mice to which our neighbours were reduced, the
sufferings so heroically borne.   Every memory
of the past rose up to incite us to make some
effort to come to the assistance of our poor old

friend; and at last it occurred to me to ask
Baroness Meyer de Rothschild, who was always
ready with good help for others, whether it
would be possible to communicate with my
besieged old lady.

I do not know by what means—perhaps if I
knew, I ought not to say—how it was that com-
munications had been established between the
English Rothschilds and those who were still in
Paris. Some trusty and devoted retainer, some
Porthos belonging to the house, had been able
to get into Paris carrying letters and messages
and food, and he was, so the Baroness now told
me, about to return again. By this means I was
told that I might send my letters and a draft on
the bank in Paris, so that poor Madame could
obtain a little help, of which she must be in
cruel need; and this being accomplished, the
letter written and the money sent off, I was able
with an easier mind to enjoy my own share of
the good things of life. Time passed, the siege
was raised, and then came a day when, urged
by circumstances, and perhaps also by a certain
curiosity, I found myself starting for Paris with
a friend, under the escort of Mr. Cook, arriving

after a night's journey through strange and
never-to-be-forgotten experiences at the Gare
du Nord—a deserted station among streets all
empty and silent.   Carriages were no longer to
be seen, every figure was dressed in black, and
the women's sad faces and long, floating crape
veils seemed strangely symbolical and visionary,
as I walked along to the house of my father's
cousin, Charlotte R., who had been my friend
ever since I could remember.   She was expecting me in her home, to which she had only been
able to return a few days before.   It is not my
purpose here to describe the strange and
pathetic experiences and the sights we saw together during that most eventful week; the
sunshine of it all, the smoking ruins, the piteous
histories, the strange rebound of life even in
the midst of its ashes: the Arc itself was
wrapped in sackcloth to preserve the impassive
gods from the injuries of war.   The great legs
and arms were packed in straw and sawdust to
protect them.   One of my first questions was
for Madame.   "She is particularly well," said
my cousin, smiling.   "She has added many
thrilling histories to her *répertoire*, Madame

Martin's escape from the *obus*, Bibi's horror of
the Prussians—you must come and see her,
and hear it all for yourself." " I particularly
want to see her," said I.   I was in a self-satisfied
and not unnatural frame of mind, picturing my
old lady's pleasure at the meeting, her eloquent
emotion and satisfaction at the trouble I had
taken on her behalf.   I hoped to have saved
her life ; at all events, I felt that she must owe
many little comforts to my exertions, and that
her grateful benediction awaited me !

Dear old Madame was sitting with her
poodle on her knees in the same little dark and
crowded chamber.   She put down her spectacles,
shut up her book—I do believe it was still the
little black History of France.   She did not
look in the least surprised to see me walk in.
The room smelt of snuff just as usual ; Bibi
leapt up from her lap, barking furiously.   "Ah !
my dear child," said the old lady calmly, "how
do you do?   Ah, my dear Miss R., I am
delighted to see you again !   Only this day I
said to Madame Martin, ' I think Miss R. will be
sure to call this afternoon, it is some day since
she come.' "   Then turning to me, " Well, my

dear A., and how do you, and how do you all?
Are you come to stay in our poor Paris? Are
Mr. and Mrs. S. with you? Oh! oh! Oh,
those Prussians! those abominable monsters!
My poor Bibi, he was ready to tear them to
pieces; he and I could not sleep for the guns.
Madame Martin, she say to me, 'Oh! Madame,
can you believe such wickedness?' I say to
her, 'It is abominable.' Oh! there is no word
for it!"

All this was oddly familiar, and yet strangely
thrilling and unreal as was all the rest. There
is no adequate expression for the strange waking nightmare which seems to seize one when
by chance one meets a whole country suffering
from one overpowering idea, and when one
hears the story of each individual experience
in turn repeated and repeated.

At last, my own personal interests rising up
again, I said, not without some curiosity: "And
now I want to ask you, did you get my letter,
Madame, and did you receive the money safely
from Messrs. Rothschilds' bank?"

"I thank you, my dear child. I received it
—I was about to mention the subject—I knew

you would not forget your old friend," said Madame solemnly. " I needed the money very much," with a shake of the head. " I was all the more grateful that it came at the time it did. You will be gratified, I know, to learn the use to which I put it. They had come round to every house in the street only that morning. Madame Martin was with me." Here Madame took a pinch of snuff very seriously. " She go to the banker's for me, and she took the money at once and inscribe my name on the list."

" The list!" said I, much bewildered.

" I subscribe it," said Madame, "to the cannon which was presented by our *quartier* to the city of Paris."

" What, all of it?" said I.

" Yes, all of it," said she. " Do you suppose I should have kept any of it back?"

CHAPTER V

MY WITCHES' CALDRON

It happily does not always follow that one cares for an author in exact proportion to the sale of his books, or even to the degree of their merit; otherwise some authors might be overpowered by friends, and others remain solitary all their lives long. It also does not always follow that people who write books are those who see most of one another. On the contrary, authors as a rule, I think, prefer playmates of other professions and don't keep together in the same way that soldiers do, for instance, or dandies, or doctors, or lawyers, or members of Parliament. Lawyers, politicians, soldiers, and even doctors, do a great deal of their work together in one another's company; but the hours don't suit for literary people, and one

rarely hears of five or six authors sitting down
in a row to write books in company. They are
generally shut up apart in different studies, with
strict orders given that nobody is to be shown
in.

This was my father's rule, only it was
constantly broken ; and many persons used to
pass in and out during his working-times,
coming to consult him or to make suggestions ;
some came to call, others brought little poems
and articles for the *Cornhill*. . . . As I write
on, it seems to me that my memory is a sort of
Witches' Caldron, from which rise one by one
these figures of the past, and they go by in
turn and vanish one by one into the mist,—
some are kings and queens in their own right,
some are friends, some are dependents. From
my caldron rise many figures, some of whom I
have looked upon once only, and then
realised in after life from a different point of
view. Now perhaps looking back, one can tell
their worth better than at the time ; one knows
which were the true companions, which were
the teachers and spiritual pastors, which were
but shadows after all. The most splendid

person I ever remember seeing had a little
pencil sketch in his hand, which he left behind
him upon the table. It was a very feeble
sketch; it seemed scarcely possible that so
grand a being should not be a bolder draughts-
man. He appeared to us one Sunday morning
in the sunshine. I came down to breakfast,
found him sitting beside my father at the table,
with an untasted cup of tea before him; he
seemed to fill the bow-window with radiance as
if he were Apollo; he leant against his chair
with one elbow resting on its back, with shining
studs and curls and boots. We could see his
horse looking in at us over the blind. It was
indeed a sight for little girls to remember all
their lives. I think my father had a certain
weakness for dandies, those knights of the
broadcloth and shining fronts. Magnificent
apparitions used to dawn upon us in the hall,
glorious beings ascended the stairs on their
way to the study, but this one outshone them
all. Our visitor was Count D'Orsay, of whom
Lord Lamington says:

When he appeared in the perfection of dress (for the
tailor's art had not died out with George IV.), with that

expression of self-confidence and complacency which the sense of superiority gives, he was the observed of all! In those days men took great pains with themselves, they did not slouch and moon thro' life. . . . I have frequently ridden down to Richmond with Count D'Orsay; a striking figure he was; his blue coat, thrown well back to show the wide expanse of snowy shirt-front, his buff waistcoat, his light leathers and polished boots, his well-curled whiskers and handsome countenance; a wide-brimmed glossy hat, and spotless white gloves.

Mr. Richard Doyle, too, used to tell us a little story of a well-known literary man who was so carried away by the presence of the brilliant D'Orsay at some City banquet, that in his enthusiasm he was heard to call aloud, above the din of voices, in a sort of burst of enthusiasm, "Waiter! for heaven's sake, bring melted butter for the Flounder of the Count!" The Count must have been well used to melted butter as he proceeded on his triumphant road, nor did his genius fail him to the last. I have read somewhere a curious description of the romantic sarcophagus he finally devised for himself in a sort of temple, a flight of marble steps leading to a marble shrine where he was duly laid when he died, not long after his return to his own country and to the land of his

fathers. He is of that race with Byron who lived
in the beginning of the century, magnificent
performers of life's commonplaces. There is a
certain absence of the florid, a frozen coldness
in the fashion of to-day which strikes those
who remember the more flamboyant generation.

I remember a visit from another hero of
those times. We were walking across Kensington Square early one morning, when we
heard some one hurrying after us and calling
my father by his name. This was also one of
Byron's friends. A bright-eyed, active old
man, with long wavy white hair and a picturesque cloak flung over one shoulder. I can see
him still, as he crossed the corner of the square
and followed us with a light rapid step. My
father, stopping short, turned back to meet
him, greeting him kindly and bringing him
home with us to the old brown house at the
corner where we were then living. There was
a sort of eagerness and vividness of manner
about the stranger which was very impressive.
You could not help watching him and his cloak,
which kept slipping from its place, and which
he caught at again and again. We wondered

at his romantic, foreign looks, and his gaiety
and bright eager way. Afterwards we were
told that this was Leigh Hunt. We knew his
name very well, for on the drawing-room table
in company with various Ruskins and Punches
lay a pretty shining book called *A Jar of
Honey from Mount Hybla*, from which, in that
dilettante childish fashion which is half-play
half-impatience and search for something else,
we had contrived to extract our own allowance
of honey. It was still an event to see a real
author in those days, specially an author with a
long cloak flung over his shoulder; though, for
the matter of that, it is still and always will be
an event to see the faces and hear the voices of
those whose thoughts have added something
delightful to our lives. Not very long afterwards came a different visitor, still belonging
to that same company of people. I had thrown
open the dining-room door and come in looking
for something, and then I stopped short, for the
room was not empty. A striking and somewhat alarming-looking person stood alone by
the fire-place with folded arms; a dark
impressive-looking man, not tall, but broad and

brown and weather-beaten, gazing with a sort
of scowl at his own reflection in the glass.   As
I entered he turned slowly and looked at me
over his shoulder.   This was Trelawny, who
had come to see my father.   He frowned,
walked deliberately and slowly from the room,
and I saw him no more.

As I have said, all these people now seem
almost like figures out of a fairy tale.   One
could almost as well imagine Sinbad, or Prince
Charming,   or   the   Seven   Champions   of
Christendom dropping in for an hour's chat.
But each generation, however matter-of-fact it
may be, sets up fairy figures in turn, to wonder
at and delight in.   I had not then read any of
the books which have since appeared, though I
had heard my elders talking, and I knew from
hearsay something of the strange, pathetic,
irrational histories of these bygone wanderers
searching the world for the Golden Fleece and
the Enchanted Gardens.   These were the only
members of that special, impracticable, romantic
crew of Argonauts I ever saw, though I have
read their histories and diaries so that I seem to
know them all, and can almost hear their voices.

One of the most notable persons who ever came into our old bow-windowed drawing-room in Young Street is a guest never to be forgotten by me, a tiny, delicate, little person, whose small hand nevertheless grasped a mighty lever which set all the literary world of that day vibrating. I can still see the scene quite plainly!—the hot summer evening, the open windows, the carriage driving to the door as we all sat silent and expectant; my father, who rarely waited, waiting with us; our governess and my sister and I all in a row, and prepared for the great event. We saw the carriage stop, and out of it sprang the active, well-knit figure of young Mr. George Smith, who was bringing Miss Brontë to see our father. My father, who had been walking up and down the room, goes out into the hall to meet his guests, and then after a moment's delay the door opens wide, and the two gentlemen come in, leading a tiny, delicate, serious, little lady, pale, with fair straight hair, and steady eyes. She may be a little over thirty; she is dressed in a little *barège* dress with a pattern of faint green moss. She enters in mittens, in silence, in seriousness; our hearts are beating with wild excitement. This then is the authoress, the unknown power whose books have set all London talking, reading, speculating; some people even say our father wrote the books—the wonderful books. To say that we little girls had been given *Jane Eyre* to read scarcely represents the facts of the case; to say that we had taken it without leave, read bits here and read bits there, been carried away by an undreamed-of and hitherto un-imagined whirlwind into things, times, places, all utterly absorbing and at the same time absolutely unintelligible to us, would more accurately describe our states of mind on that summer's evening as we look at Jane Eyre— the great Jane Eyre—the tiny little lady. The moment is so breathless that dinner comes as a relief to the solemnity of the occasion, and we all smile as my father stoops to offer his arm; for, genius though she may be, Miss Brontë can barely reach his elbow. My own personal impressions are that she is somewhat grave and stern, specially to forward little girls who wish to chatter; Mr. George Smith has since told me how she afterwards remarked upon my father's wonderful forbearance and gentleness with our uncalled-for incursions into the conversation. She sat gazing at him with kindling eyes of interest; lighting up with a sort of illumination every now and then as she answered him. I can see her bending forward over the table, not eating, but listening to what he said as he carved the dish before him.

I think it must have been on this very occasion that my father invited some of his friends in the evening to meet Miss Brontë— for everybody was interested and anxious to see her. Mrs. Crowe, the reciter of ghost-stories, was there. Mrs. Brookfield, Mrs. Carlyle, Mr. Carlyle himself was present, so I am told, railing at the appearance of cockneys upon Scotch mountain sides; there were also too many Americans for his taste, "but the Americans were as gods compared to the cockneys," says the philosopher. Besides the Carlyles, there were Mrs. Elliott and Miss Perry, Mrs. Procter and her daughter, most of my father's habitual friends and companions. In the recent life of Lord Houghton I was amused to see a note quoted in which Lord Houghton also was convened. Would that he had been present!—perhaps the party would have gone off better. It was a gloomy and a silent evening. Every one waited for the brilliant conversation which never began at all. Miss Brontë retired to the sofa in the study, and murmured a low word now and then to our kind governess, Miss Truelock. The room looked very dark, the lamp began to smoke a little, the conversation grew dimmer and more dim, the ladies sat round still expectant, my father was too much perturbed by the gloom and the silence to be able to cope with it at all. Mrs. Brookfield, who was in the doorway by the study, near the corner in which Miss Brontë was sitting, leant forward with a little commonplace, since brilliance was not to be the order of the evening. "Do you like London, Miss Brontë?" she said; another silence, a pause, then Miss Brontë answers, "Yes and No" very gravely; Mrs. Brookfield has herself reported the conversation. My sister and I were much too young to be bored in those days; alarmed, impressed we might be, but not yet bored. A party was a party, a lioness was a lioness; and—shall I confess it?—at that time an extra dish of biscuits was enough to mark the evening. We felt all the importance of the occasion; tea spread in the dining-room, ladies in the drawing-room; we roamed about inconveniently, no doubt, and excitedly, and in one of my excursions crossing the hall, after Miss Brontë had left I was surprised to see my father opening the front door with his hat on. He put his fingers to his lips, walked out into the darkness, and shut the door quietly behind him. When I went back to the drawing-room again, the ladies asked me where he was. I vaguely answered that I thought he was coming back. I was puzzled at the time, nor was it all made clear to me till long years afterwards, when one day Mrs. Procter asked me if I knew what had happened once when my father had invited a party to meet Jane Eyre at his house. It was one of the dullest evenings she had ever spent in her life, she said. And then with a good deal of humour she described the situation—the ladies who had all come expecting so much delightful conversation, and the gloom and the constraint, and how finally, overwhelmed by the situation, my father had quietly left the room, left the house, and gone off to his club. The ladies waited, wondered, and finally departed also; and as we were going up to bed with our candles after everybody was gone, I remember two pretty Miss L.'s, in shiny silk dresses, arriving, full of expectation. . . . We still said we thought our father would soon be back, but the Miss L.'s declined to wait upon the chance, laughed, and drove away again almost immediately.

Since writing the preceding lines, I have visited Jane Eyre land, and stayed in the delightful home where she used to stay with Mrs. Gaskell. I have seen signs and tokens of her presence, faint sketches vanishing away, the delicate writing in the beautiful books she gave that warm friend; and I have also looked for and re-read the introduction to *Emma*, that "last sketch" and most touching chapter in the never-to-be-written book of Charlotte Brontë's happy married life. The paper is signed "W.

M. T."; it was written by the editor, and is printed in one of the very earliest numbers of the *Cornhill Magazine*.

I remember the trembling little frame, the little hand, the great honest eyes; an impetuous honesty seemed to me to characterise the woman. . . . I fancied an austere little Joan of Arc marching in upon us and rebuking our easy lives, our easy morals. She gave me the impression of being a very pure and lofty and high-minded person. A great and holy reverence of right and truth seemed to be with her always. Such in our brief interview she appeared to me. As one thinks of that life, so noble, so lonely—of that passion for truth—of those nights and nights of eager study, swarming fancies, invention, depression, elation, and prayer; as one reads of the necessarily incomplete though most touching and admirable history of the heart that throbbed in this one little frame—of this one among the myriads of souls that have lived and died on this great earth—this great earth!—this little speck in the infinite universe of God, with what wonder do we think of to-day, with what awe await to-morrow, when that which is now but darkly seen shall be clear?

As I write out what my father's hand has written my gossip is hushed, and seems to me like the lamp-smoke in the old drawing-room compared to the light of the summer's night in the street outside.

CHAPTER VI

MY WITCHES' CALDRON—II

I AM suddenly conscious as I write that my
experiences are very partial; but a witch's
caldron must needs after all contain hetero-
geneous scraps; and mine, alas! can be no
exception to the rest. It produces nothing
more valuable than odds and ends happily
harmless enough, neither sweltered venom nor
fillet of finny snake, but the back of one great
man's head, the hat and umbrella of another.
The first time I ever saw Mr. Gladstone I only
saw the soles of his boots. A friend had taken
me into the ventilator of the House of Commons,
where we listened to a noble speech and
watched the two shadows on the grating overhead of the feet of the messenger of glad tidings.
One special *back* I cannot refrain from writing

down, in a dark blue frock coat and strapped
trousers, walking leisurely before us up
Piccadilly. The sun is shining, and an odd
sort of brass buckle which fastens an old-
fashioned stock, flashes like a star. "Do
look!" I say to my father. "Who is that old
gentleman?" "That old gentleman! Why,
that is the Duke of Wellington," said my father.
On another occasion I remember some one
coming up to us and beginning to talk very
charmingly, and among other things describing
some new Lord Mayor who had been in state to
a theatrical performance, by which it seemed
he had been much affected. "I cried, I do
assure you," the Lord Mayor had said, "and as
for the Lady Mayoress, she cry too"; and the
gentleman smiled and told the little story so
dryly and drolly that my sister and I couldn't
help laughing, and we went on repeating to one
another afterwards, "As for the Lady Mayoress,
she cry too." And then as usual we asked who
was that. "Don't you know Lord Palmerston
by sight?" says my father.

I have a friend who declares that Fate is a
humorist, linking us all together by strangest

whims, even by broad jokes at times; and this vague little humour of the weeping Lady Mayoress is my one personal link with the great Whig administrator of the last generation.

Another miscellaneous apparition out of my caldron rises before me as I write. On a certain day we went to call at Mrs. Procter's with our father. We found an old man standing in the middle of the room, taking leave of his hostess, nodding his head—he was a little like a Chinese mandarin with an ivory face. His expression never changed but seemed quite fixed. He knew my father and spoke to him and to us too, still in this odd fixed way. Then he looked at my sister. "My little girl," he said to her, "will you come and live with me? You shall be as happy as the day is long; you shall have a white pony to ride, and feed upon red-currant jelly." This prospect was so alarming and unexpected that the poor little girl suddenly blushed up and burst into tears. The old man was Mr. Samuel Rogers, but happily he did not see her cry, for he was already on his way to the door.

My father was very fond of going to the

play, and he used to take us when we were
children, one on each side of him, in a hansom.
He used to take us to the opera too, which was
less of a treat.   Magnificent envelopes, with
unicorns and heraldic emblazonments, used to
come very constantly, containing tickets and
boxes for the opera.   In those days we thought
everybody had boxes for the opera as a matter
of course.   We used to be installed in the front
places with our chins resting on the velvet
ledges of the box.   For a time it used to be
very delightful, then sometimes I used suddenly
to wake up to find the singing still going on
and on as in a dream.   I can still see Lablache,
a huge reverberating mountain, a sort of
Olympus, thundering forth glorious sounds, and
addressing deep resounding notes to what
seemed to me then a sort of fairy in white.
She stood on tiny feet, she put up a delicate
finger and sent forth a sweet vibration of song
in answer, sweeter, shriller, more charming
every instant.   Did she fly right up into the
air, or was it my own head that came down
with a sleepy nod ?   I slept, I awoke ; and each
time I was conscious of this exquisite floating

ripple of music flowing in and out of my dreams.
The singer was Mademoiselle Sontag ; it was
the *Elisire*, or some such opera, overflowing
like a lark's carol.   All the great golden house
applauded ; my father applauded.   I longed to
hear more, but in vain I struggled, I only
slumbered again, waking from minute to minute
to see the lovely little lady in white still standing there, still pouring forth her melody to
the thousand lights and people.   I find when I
consult my faithful *confidante* and sympathiser
in these small memories of what is now so
nearly forgotten, that I am not alone in my
admiring impressions of this charming person.
My *confidante* is the *Biographie Générale*,
where I find an account, no sleepy visionary
impression, such as my own, but a very definite
and charming portrait of the bright fairy of my
dreams, of Mademoiselle Sontag, Comtesse
Rossi, who came to London in 1849 :—" On
rémarquait surtout la limpidité de ses gammes
chromatiques et l'éclat de ses trilles . . . Et
toutes ces merveilles s'accomplissaient avec une
grâce parfaite, sans que le regard fût jamais
attristé par le moindre effort.   La figure

charmante de Mademoiselle Sontag, ses beaux
yeux bleus, limpides et doux, ses formes
élégantes, sa taille élancée et souple achevaient
le tableau et complétaient l'enchantement."

It seems sad to have enjoyed this delightful
performance only in one's dreams, but under
these humiliating circumstances when the whole
world was heaving and struggling to hear the
great singer of the North, and when the usual
box arrived for the *Figlia del Reggimento*, my
grandmother, who was with us, invited two
friends of her own, grown up and accustomed
to keep awake, and my sister and I were not
included in the party. We were not disappointed, we *imagined* the songs for ourselves
as children do. We gathered all our verbenas
and geraniums for a nosegay and gave it to our
guests to carry, and watched the carriage roll
off in the twilight with wild hopes, unexpressed,
that perhaps the flowers would be cast upon
the stage at the feet of the great singer. But
though the flowers returned home again crushed
and dilapidated, and though we did not hear
the song, it was a reality for me and lasted
until a day, long years after, when I heard that

stately and glorious voice flashing into my
darkness with a shock of amazement never to
be forgotten, and then and there realised how
futile an imagination may be.

Alas! I never possessed a note of music of
my own, though I have cared for it in a patient,
unrequited way all my life long. My father
always loved music and understood it too; he
knew his opera tunes by heart. I have always
liked the little story of his landing with his
companions at Malta on his way to the East,
and as no one of the company happened to
speak Italian he was able to interpret for the
whole party by humming lines from various
operas, "'Un biglietto—Eccolo quà,'" says my
father to the man from the shore, "'Lascu
darem' la mano,'" and he helped Lady T. up
the gangway, and so on. He used sometimes
to bring Mr. Ella home to dine with him, and
he liked to hear his talk about music. Through
Mr. Ella's kindness the doors of the Musical
Union flew open wide to us.

My father used to write in his study at the
back of the house in Young Street. The vine
shaded his two windows, which looked out

upon the bit of garden, and the medlar tree,
and the Spanish jessamines of which the yellow
flowers scented our old brick walls. I can
remember the tortoise belonging to the boys
next door crawling along the top of the wall
where they had set it, and making its way
between the jessamine sprigs. Jessamines
won't grow now any more, as they did then, in
the gardens of Kensington, nor will medlars
and vine trees take root and spread their green
branches; only herbs and bulbs, such as lilies
and Solomon seals, seem to flourish, though I
have a faint hope that all the things people put
in will come up all right some centuries hence,
when London is resting and at peace, and has
turned into the grass-grown ruin one so often
hears described. Our garden was not tidy
(though on one grand occasion a man came to
mow the grass), but it was full of sweet things.
There were verbenas—red, blue, and scented;
and there were lovely stacks of flags, blades of
green with purple heads between, and bunches
of London Pride growing luxuriantly; and
there were some blush roses at the end of the
garden, which were not always quite eaten up

by the caterpillars. Lady Duff Gordon came
to stay with us once (it was on that occasion, I
think, that the grass was mowed), and she afterwards sent us some doves, which used to hang
high up in a wicker cage from the windows of
the schoolroom. The top schoolroom was over
my father's bedroom, and the bedroom was
over the study where he used to write. I liked
the top schoolroom the best of all the rooms in
the dear old house, the sky was in it and the
evening bells used to ring into it across the
garden, and seemed to come in dancing and
clanging with the sunset; and the floor sloped
so, that if you put down a ball it would roll in a
leisurely way right across the room of its own
accord. And then there was a mystery—a
small trap-door between the windows which we
never could open. Where did not that trap-
door lead to! It was the gateway of Paradise,
of many paradises to us. We kept our dolls,
our bricks, our books, our baby-houses in the
top room, and most of our stupid little fancies.
My little sister had a menagerie of snails and
flies in the sunny window-sill; these latter,
chiefly invalids rescued out of milk-jugs, lay

upon rose - leaves in various little pots and receptacles. She was very fond of animals, and so was my father—at least he always liked *our* animals. Now, looking back, I am full of wonder at the number of cats we were allowed to keep, though De la Pluche, the butler, and Gray, the housekeeper, waged war against them. The cats used to come to us from the garden, for then, as now, the open spaces of Kensington abounded in fauna. My sister used to adopt and christen them all in turn by the names of her favourite heroes; she had Nicholas Nickleby, a huge gray tabby, and Martin Chuzzlewit, and a poor little half-starved Barnaby Rudge, and many others. Their saucers used to be placed in a row on the little terrace at the back of my father's study, under the vine where the sour green grapes grew— not at all out of reach; and at the farther end of which was an empty greenhouse ornamented by the busts of my father as a boy, and of a relation in a military cloak.

One of my friends—she never lived to be an old woman—used to laugh and say that she had reached the time of life when she loved to

see even the people her parents had particularly
disliked, just for the sake of old times. I don't
know how I should feel if I were to meet one
agreeable, cordial gentleman, who used to come
on horseback and invite us to all sorts of
dazzling treats and entertainments, which, to
our great disappointment, my father invariably
refused, saying, "No, I don't like him; I don't
want to have anything to do with him." The
wretched man fully justified these objections by
getting himself transported long after for a
protracted course of peculiarly deliberate and
cold-blooded fraud. On one occasion a friend
told me he was talking to my father, and
mentioning some one in good repute at the
time, my father incidentally spoke as if he
knew of a murder that person had committed.
"You know it, then!" said the other man.
"Who could have told you?" My father had
never been told, but he had known it all along,
he said; and indeed he sometimes spoke of this
curious feeling he had about people at times, as
if uncomfortable facts in their past history were
actually revealed to him. At the same time I
do not think anybody had a greater enjoyment

than he in other people's goodness and well-doing; he used to be proud of a boy's prizes at school, he used to be proud of a woman's sweet voice or of her success in housekeeping. He had a friend in the Victoria Road hard by whose delightful household ways he used to describe, and I can still hear the lady he called "Jingleby" warbling "O du schöne Müllerin," to his great delight. Any generous thing or word seemed like something happening to himself. I can remember, when *David Copperfield* came out, hearing him saying with emphasis to my grandmother that "little Em'ly's letter to old Peggotty was a masterpiece." I wondered to hear him at the time, for that was not at all the part I cared for most, nor indeed could I imagine how little Em'ly ever was so stupid as to run away from Peggotty's enchanted house-boat. But we each and all enjoyed in turn our share of those thin green books full of delicious things, and how glad we were when they came to our hands at last, after our elders and our governess and our butler had all read them in turn.

It is curious to me now to remember, considering how little we met and what a long way off they lived, what an important part the Dickens household played in our childhood. But the Dickens books were as much a part of our home as our own father's.

Certainly the Dickens children's parties were shining facts in our early London days—nothing came in the least near them. There were other parties, and they were very nice, but nothing to compare to these; not nearly so light, not nearly so shining, not nearly so going round and round. Perhaps it was not all as brilliantly wonderful as I imagined it, but most assuredly the spirit of mirth and kindly jollity was a reality to every one present, and the master of the house had that wondrous fairy gift of leadership. I know not what to call that power by which he inspired every one with spirit and interest. One special party I remember, which seemed to me to go on for years with its kind, gay hospitality, its music, its streams of children passing and re-passing. We were a little shy coming in alone in all the consciousness of new shoes and ribbons, but Mrs. Dickens called us to sit beside her till the

long sweeping dance was over, and talked to
us as if we were grown up, which is always
flattering to little girls.   Then Miss Hogarth
found us partners, and we too formed part of
the throng.   I remember watching the white
satin shoes and long flowing white sashes of
the little Dickens girls, who were just about
our own age, but how much more graceful and
beautifully dressed.   Our sashes were bright
plaids of red and blue, a tribute from one of our
father's Scotch admirers (is it ungrateful to
confess now after all these years that we could
not bear them?); our shoes were only bronze.
Shall I own to this passing shadow, amid all
that radiance?   But when people are once
dancing they are all equal again and happy.

Somehow after the music we all floated into
a long supper-room, and I found myself sitting
near the head of the table by Mr. Dickens,
with another little girl much younger than myself; she wore a necklace and pretty little
sausage curls all round her head.   Mr. Dickens
was very kind to the little girl, and presently I
heard him persuading her to sing, and he put
his arm round her to encourage her; and then,

wonderful to say, the little girl stood up (she was little Miss Hullah) and began very shyly, trembling and blushing at first, but as she blushed and trembled she sang more and more sweetly: and then all the *jeunesse dorée*, consisting of the little Dickens boys and their friends, ranged along the supper table, clapped and clapped, and Mr. Dickens clapped too, smiling and applauding. And then he made a little speech, with one hand on the table; I think it was thanking the *jeunesse dorée* for their applause, and they again clapped and laughed—but here my memory fails me, and everything grows very vague.

Only this much I do remember very clearly, that we had danced and supped and danced again; and that we were all standing in a hall lighted and hung with bunches of Christmas green, and, as I have said, everything seemed altogether magnificent and important, more magnificent and important every minute, as the evening went on, and more and more people kept arriving. The hall was crowded, and the broad staircase was lined with little boys —thousands of little boys whose heads and

legs and arms were waving about together.
They were making a great noise, and shouting,
and the eldest son of the house seemed to be
marshalling them.   Presently their noise became a cheer, and then another, and we looked
up and saw that our own father had come to
fetch us, and that his white head was there
above the others ; then came a third final ringing cheer, and some one went up to him—it
was Mr. Dickens himself—who laughed and
said quickly, " That is for you ! " and my father
looked up surprised, pleased, touched, settled
his spectacles and nodded gravely to the little
boys.

CHAPTER VII

Ours was more or less a bachelor's establish-
ment, and the arrangements of the house varied
between a certain fastidiousness and the
roughest simplicity. We had shabby table-
cloths, alternating with some of my grandmother's fine linen ; we had old Derby china for
our dessert of dried figs and dry biscuits, and a
silver Flaxman teapot (which always poured
oblations of tea upon the cloth) for breakfast,
also three cracked cups and saucers of unequal
patterns and sizes. One morning, Jeames de
la Pluche (so my father's servant and factotum
chose to call himself when he wrote to the
papers) brought in a hamper which had just
arrived. When it was unpacked we found, to
our great satisfaction, that it contained a lovely

breakfast array. A china bowl for my father's
tea, ornamented with his initials in gold amid a
trellis of roses; beautiful cups for the young
ladies, lovely gilt milk-jugs, and a copy of verses,
not written, but put together out of printed
letters from the *Times*. I quote it from memory :

> Of esteem as a token,—
> Fate preserve it unbroken—
> A friend sends this tea-dish of porcelain rare.
> And with truth and sincerity
> Wishes health and prosperity
> To the famed M. A. Titmarsh of *Vanity Fair*.

We could not imagine who the friend was
from whom the opportune present had come.
For many breakfasts we speculated and
wondered, guessing one person and another in
turn, while we sat at our now elegant board, of
which Dr. Oliver Holmes himself might have
approved. Years afterwards, when De la
Pluche was taking leave of my father and
sailing for Australia, where he had obtained a
responsible position, he said, reproachfully :
" I sent you the breakfast things ; you guessed
a great many people, but you never guessed
they came from me."

De la Pluche was devoted to my father, and

next to him he seemed the most important member of the household. He was more than devoted. We used to think he was a sorcerer. He used to guess at my father's thoughts, plan for him, work for him, always knew beforehand what he would like far better than we ever did. I remember that we almost cried on one occasion, thinking that our father would ultimately prefer him to us. He used to write to the papers, and sign his letters, " Jeames de la Pluche, 13 Young Street." " Like to see my last, miss ? " he used to say, as he put down a paper on the schoolroom table. He was a very good and clever man, though a stern ruler. My father had a real friendship and regard for him, and few of his friends ever deserved it more. He lived alone downstairs, where he was treated with great deference, and had his meals served separately, I believe. He always called my father " the Governor." He was a little man, and was very like Holbein's picture of Sir Thomas More in looks. I remember on one occasion coming away from some lecture or entertainment. As we got out into the street it was raining. " It has turned cold," said my father, who was already beginning to be ill. At that moment a voice behind him said, "Coat, sir? Brought it down"; and there was De la Pluche, who had brought his coat all the way from Kensington, helping him on with it. My father thanked him, and then mechanically felt in the pocket for a possible cigar-case. "Cigar? Here," says De la Pluche, popping one into my father's mouth, and producing a match ready lighted.

I sometimes hear from my old friend, and I hope he may not be pained by reading of these childish jealousies long past.

When we were children attending our classes we used to be encouraged to study large sheets with coloured designs representing the solar system and its various intricacies. One can understand the pictures in the book while one is looking at them, but it is a very different thing from looking at pictures, to try to understand the reality as it exists outside the print, and to stand on one's own doorstep, for instance, trying to realise it all. The earth is turning one way, and the moon corkscrewing round it, and

the planets are dancing their mighty course, and
the fixed stars disappearing at the same time
behind the opposite roof, to say nothing of a
possibility that one's feet may be up in the air
and one's head hanging down below, without
any feeling of inconvenience (except perhaps a
certain bewilderment and confusion on most
subjects, which may, however, be peculiar to
myself).   And so, looking back on one's own
life it is difficult to fit all the events and
chronologies accurately into their places.   If
one tries to realise too much at once, the
impression is apt to grow chaotic and unmean-
ing in its complexity ; you can't get the propor-
tions of events ; and, perhaps, indeed, one of
the compensating constituents of all our various
existences consists in that very disproportion
which passing impressions most happily take
for us, and which they often retain, notwithstanding the experiences of years.   That little
picture of Bewick's, in which a falling leaf
conceals the sky, the road, the passing gig and
its occupants, has always seemed to me to
contain the secret of a whole philosophy
which makes existence itself more possible,

than it would be, if infinity held its proportional
place in our finite experience. . . .

Our London home was a happy but a very
quiet home.   One day my father said that he
had been surprised to hear from his friend Sir
Henry Davison how seriously our house struck
people, compared to other houses: "But I
think we are very happy as we are," said he—
and so indeed we were.   We lived chiefly with
him and with quite little children, or with our
grandparents when they came over to visit us.
There was certainly a want of initiation: in
our house there was no one to suggest all sorts
of delightful possibilities, which, as we grew up,
might have been made more of; but looking
back, I chiefly regret it in so far as I think he
might have been happier if we had brought a
little more action and sunshine into daily life,
and taken a little more on our own responsibility,
instead of making ourselves into his shadows.

When my father had done his day's work,
he liked a change of scene and thought.   I
think he was always glad to leave the ink-blots
for his beloved dabs of paint.   Sometimes he
used to drive into town on the top of an

omnibus, sometimes in a brougham; very often
he used to take us with him in hansoms (which
we much preferred) on long expeditions to
Hampstead, to Richmond, to Greenwich, or to
studios in distant quarters of the town.   There
was Mr. David Roberts's studio; his welcome
was certain, and his sketch-books were an
unfailing delight to turn over; indeed, the
drawings were so accurate, delicate, and
suggestive, that they used to make one almost
giddy to look at.   Once or twice we went to
Mr. Cattermole's, who had a studio among the
Hampstead hills, hidden among ancient walls
and ivy-trees.   Mr. Du Maurier was not yet
living there, or I am sure we should have
driven further up the hill.   As life goes on, one
grudges that time and chance alone should
have separated people who would have been so
happy with each other.   Sometimes we used to
go to Sir Edwin Landseer's beautiful villa in
St. John's Wood, and enjoy his delightful
company.   Among his many stories (as he
stood painting at his huge canvases), I
remember his once telling us an anecdote of
one of his dogs.   He was in the habit of taking

it out every day after his work was over. The
dog used to wait patiently all day long while
Sir Edwin was painting, but he used to come
and lie down at his feet and look up in his face
towards five o'clock; and on one occasion,
finding his hints disregarded, he trotted into
the hall and came back with the painter's hat,
which he laid on the floor before him.

Then we always enjoyed going on to the
house of a neighbour of Sir Edwin's, Mr.
Charles Leslie, who dwelt somewhere in that
locality with a delightful household. To say
nothing of the actual members of that painter's
home, there were others also belonging to it
who were certainly all but alive. I can still see
my father standing in the South Kensington
Museum, sympathetic and laughing before the
picture of Sancho Panza, in which he sits with
his finger to his nose, with that look of portentous
wisdom and absurdity. As for the charming
Duchess, whose portrait is also to be seen, she,
or her prototypes, must surely have dwelt in
the painter's own home. Mr. Dickens used to
be at the Leslies' sometimes, and though I
cannot quite account for it, I have a general

impression of fireworks perpetually going off just outside their windows.

One day that we had come home from one of these expeditions in a big blue fly, with a bony horse,—it was a bright blue fly, with a drab inside to it, and an old white coachman on the box—my father, after a few words of consultation with the coachman, drove off again, and shortly afterwards returning on foot, told us that he had just bought the whole concern, brougham and horse and harness, and that he had sent Jackson (our driver had now become Jackson) to be measured for a great-coat. So henceforward we came and went about in our own private carriage, which, however, never lost its original name of "the fly," although Jackson's buttons shone resplendent with the Thackeray crest, and the horse too seemed brushed up and promoted to be private.

I remember, or I think I remember, driving in this vehicle to Mr. Frank Stone's studio in Tavistock Square, and how he and my father began laughing and talking about early days. "Do you remember that portrait I began to paint of you over the lady with the guitar?"

Mr. Stone said, and he added that he had the picture still, and, going into some deep cupboard, he brought out a cheerful florid picture of my father, as I for one had never seen him, with thick black hair and a young ruddy face. We brought it away with us, and I have it now, and the lady's red dress still appears in the background. It is perhaps fortunate that people, as a rule, are well and happy and at their best when their portraits are painted. If one looks down the Academy list year by year, one sees that the pictures represent gentlemen who have just been made Bishops, or Speakers, or Governors-General ; or ladies who are brides in their lovely new clothes and jewels. Sad folks hide their heads, sick folks turn them away, and are not fit subjects for the painter's art ; and yet, as I write, I am also conscious that facts contradict me, and that there has been a fine run of late upon nurses and death-bed scenes in general.

The happy hour had not yet come for us when Mr. Watts came to live in Kensington at Little Holland House, and built his studios there. This was in later times, and after we had just passed beyond the great pinafore age, which sets such a stamp upon after life, and to which my recollections seem chiefly to revert.

He always said that he should like to paint a picture of my father, but the day for the sitting, alas, never came! And yet I can imagine what that picture might have been,— a portrait, such as some portraits, with that mysterious reality in them, that *present* which is quite apart from time and dates.

I am sure there was no one among all his friends whose society my father enjoyed more than he did that of John Leech, whom he first remembered, so he has often told us with a smile, a small boy at the Charterhouse, in a little blue buttoned-up suit, set up upon a form and made to sing " Home, sweet home," to the others crowding round about. Mr. Leech was anything but a small boy when I remember him in the old Young Street dining-room, where De la Pluche was laying the cloth, while Mr. Leech and my father sat talking by the fire. He was very handsome and tall, and kind and shy, and he spoke in a husky, melodious voice: we admired him very much ; he was

always beautifully dressed, and we used to see
him come riding up to the door on nice shining
horses; and he generally came to invite us all
to something delightful—to go there, or to dine
with him and his wife at Richmond or elsewhere. My father liked to take us about with
him, and I am surprised, as I think of it, at the
great good-nature of his friends. who used so
constantly to include two inconvenient little
girls in the various invitations they sent him.
We used to be asked early, and to arrive at all
sorts of unusual times. We used to lunch with
our hosts and spend long afternoons, and then
about dinner-time our father would come in,
and sit smoking after dinner, while we waited
with patient ladies upstairs. Mrs. Brookfield
used to live in Portman Street in those days.
and thither we used to go very constantly. and
to Mrs. Procter's, as well as to various relations'
houses, Indian cousins of my father's coming
to town for a season with their colonels and
their families. Time after time we used to go
to the Leeches, who lived in Brunswick Square.
We used to play with the baby, we used to turn
over endless books of pictures. and perhaps go

out for a walk with kind Mrs. Leech, and sometimes (but this happened very rarely) we used
to be taken up to the room where John Leech
himself sat at his drawing-table under the
square of silver paper which softened the light
as it fell upon his blocks.   There was his back
as he bent over his work, there were the tables
loaded with picture-books and drawing-blocks,
huge blocks, four times the size of any at home,
ready for next week's *Punch;* but our entrance
disturbed him (we instinctively felt how much),
and we used to hurry quickly back to the
drawing-books downstairs, and go on turning
over the pencil sketches.   I have some of them
now, those drawings so roughly indicated, at
first so vague, and then by degrees worked
upon and altered and modelled and forced into
their life as it were, *obliged* to laugh, charmed
into kindly wit ; as I look at them now, I still
recognise the aspect of those bygone days and
places, and I cannot help thinking how much
more interesting to remember are some of the
shabby homes in which work and beauty and
fun are *made*, than those more luxurious and
elaborate, which dazzle us at the time, where

everything one saw was only bought. But after all the whole secret of life is made up of the things one makes, and those one steals, and those one pays for.

My own children turn over Leech's drawings now, as happily as we ourselves used to do, and it seems to me sometimes as if they also are at play among our own old fancies and in our old haunts. There are the rooms again. There is Mrs. Leech's old piano like an organ standing bolt upright against the wall; there are the brown holland covers on the chairs; there is the domestic lamp, looking (as the lamps of one's youth used to look) tall and dismantled like some gaunt lighthouse erected upon bare mahogany rocks. Besides these things, I remember with real affection a lovely little miniature portrait of Mrs. Leech, which used to hang upon the wall, and which was done at the time of her marriage. It was indeed the sweetest little picture; and when I saw her one little granddaughter Dorothy Gillett, this old favourite picture of my childhood came into my mind. It may be hallucination, but, although the houses were so ugly in those days, I still

think the people in them looked almost nicer
then than they do now.

Madame Elise was the great oracle of the
'Fifties, and she used to turn out floating,
dignified, squashy beings with close pearly
head-dresses and bonnets, and sloping, spreading draperies.   They are all to be seen in Mr.
Leech's pictures still, and they may be about
to come back to life, crinolines and all, for
anything I know to the contrary.   But I hope
not; I think this present generation of women
is a happier one than that one was.   The
characters of the people I remember were
certainly different from the characters of their
daughters of the present, disporting themselves in the golden Du Maurier age of
liberty and out-door life.   Mr. Leech once
drew our own green curtains for us in a
little picture of two girls asking a child what
it had for dinner.   The child says, " Something that begins with a S."; and when asked
what that might be, explains that it was *cold
beef.*

A certain number of writers and designers
for *Punch* used to dine at Mr. Leech's, coming

in with my father towards the close of the day.
I remember Mr. Tenniel there, and Mr. Percival
Legh, and Mr. Shirley Brooks, and Millais in
later days, and an eminent member of a different
profession, the present Dean of Rochester.
Sometimes, instead of dining in Brunswick
Square or at the house in Kensington (to
which they afterwards removed), we used to be
taken all away to Richmond, to enjoy happy
hours upon the terrace, and the light of setting
suns.

My father was pleased when some dozen
years later the Leeches came to Kensington,
and he was greatly interested in their pretty
old house.   Mr. Leech was pleased too ; and
at first he used to describe with resigned humour
what, alas, became slow torture in the end to
his strained nerves,—the different noises as
they succeeded each other in what he had expected to find a quiet suburb of London : the
milkman, the carrier, the industrious carpenter,
all following in rotation one by one, from the
very earliest morning.   But his nerves were
altogether overstrung.   I remember hearing

him once, in far, far back times, tell a little
story, scarcely perhaps worth retelling. He
was looking altogether ill and upset, and he
told us that he had hardly recovered from a
little shock the night before. Coming home
late, and as he went upstairs, he had been
annoyed by hearing the howling of a dog in
a garden at the back of the house. He did
not know that one of his young sisters had
come to see his wife that evening, had been
persuaded to stay for the night, and put to
sleep in the very room into which he now
turned, throwing up the window to see where
the noise came from. The moon was shining,
and happening to look round he was quite
overcome, seeing a figure lying motionless
upon the bed, while the light poured coldly
upon a white marble profile.

I was going along the Kensington Road
towards Palace Green one fine morning, when
I met my father carefully carrying before him
two blue Dutch china pots, which he had just
surreptitiously taken away out of his own study.
" I am going to see if they won't stand upon
Leech's dining-room chimney-piece," he said.

I followed him, hoping, I am afraid, that they would not stand there, for we were well used to lament the accustomed disappearance of his pretty ornaments and china dishes. People may have stared to see him carrying his china, but that I do not now remember,—only this, that he was amused and interested, and that we found the iron gates open to the court in front, and the doors of the Leeches' house all wide open, though the house itself was empty and the family had not yet arrived. Workmen were coming and going, busy hammering carpets and making arrangements. We crossed the hall, and then my father led the way into the pretty old dining-room, with its new Turkey carpet and its tall windows looking to the gardens at the back. "I knew they would stand there," said he, putting up the two blue pots on the high narrow ledge; and there to my mind they will ever stand. . . .[1]

It was in the *Quarterly Review* that my father wrote of Leech's pictures. "While we live we must laugh," he says.

Do we laugh enough? Our fathers laughed

[1] Midsummer 1894.—Kensington Terrace has been pulled down.

better than we do. Is it that we have over-
eaten of the fruit of the tree of knowledge ? I
cannot say. The art of design, as practised by
the successors of John Leech who have followed
in his steps, still holds its own delightful sway ;
but the kindred arts of action, of oratory, of
literature, have, to some narrow-minded critics,
taken most unpleasant forms of sincerity. Sometimes I wonder how the moralist would write
of us now, were he still among us. I don't
know how the present will strike the new
generation, when it has grown up to look back
in turn upon this somewhat complicated phase
of civilisation. Sheep's clothing is out of date,
and wolf-skins all the fashion now; but they
are imitation wolf-skins. The would-be Lion
affects the Donkey's ears; the Pharisee is
anxious to be seen in the Publican's society for
the good impression it makes upon his constit-
uency. It is all very perplexing, and not very
edifying to speculate on. And then I feel that
any day, while one is fumbling and probing
and dissecting and splitting hairs, some genius
such as John Leech's silently appears, and
touches commonplace things, and lo! here is

a new light upon earth, a new happiness;
here is another smile in the land. "Can
we have too much of truth and fun and
beauty and kindness?" said John Leech's
Friend.

CHAPTER VIII

TO WEIMAR AND BACK

I SUPPOSE the outer circuit of my own very limited wanderings must have been reached at the age of thirteen, or thereabouts, when my father took me and my little sister for the grand tour of Europe. We had of course lived in Paris and spent our summers in quiet sunny country places abroad with our grandparents, but this was to be something different from anything we had ever known before at St. Germains or Montmorenci among the donkeys; Switzerland, and Venice, and Vienna, Germany and the Rhine! our young souls thrilled with expectation. And yet those early feasts of life are not unlike the miracle of the loaves and fishes; the twelve basketfuls that remain in after years are certainly even more precious than the feast itself.

We started one sleety summer morning. My father was pleased to be off, and we were enchanted. He had bought a gray wide-awake hat for the journey, and he had a new sketch-book in his pocket, besides two smaller ones for us, which he produced as the steamer was starting. We sailed from London Bridge, and the decks were all wet and slippery as we came on board. We were scatter-brained little girls, although we looked demure enough in our mushroom hats and waterproofs. We also had prepared a travelling trousseau, which consisted of miscellaneous articles belonging to the fancy goods department of things in general, rather than to the usual outfit of an English gentleman's family. I was not without some diffidence about my luggage. I remember a draught-board, a large wooden work-box, a good many books, paint-boxes, and other odds and ends; but I felt that whatever else might be deficient our *new bonnets* would bring us triumphantly out of every crisis. They were alike, but with a difference of blue and pink wreaths of acacia, and brilliant in ribbons to match. at a time when people affected less dazzling colours than

they do now. Of course these treasures were
not for the Channel and its mischances; they
were carefully packed away and guarded by the
draught-boards and work-boxes and the other
contents of our trunk; and I may as well con-
clude the episode at once, for it is not quite
without bearing upon what I am trying to
recall. Alas for human expectations! When
the happy moment came at last, and we had
reached foreign parts and issued out of the
hotel dressed and wreathed and triumphantly
splendid, my father said: " My dear children,
go back and put those bonnets away in your
box, and don't ever wear them any more! Why,
you would be mobbed in these places if you
walked out alone with such ribbons!" How
the sun shone as he spoke; how my heart sank
under the acacia trees. My sister was eleven
years old, and didn't care a bit; but at thirteen
and fourteen one's clothes begin to strike root.
I felt disgraced, beheaded of my lovely bonnet,
utterly crushed, and I turned away to hide my
tears.

Now, there is a passage in the life of Charles
Kingsley which, as I believe, concerned this

very time and journey; and I am amused, as I
remember the tragedy of my bonnet, to think of
the different sacrifices which men and women
have to pay to popular prejudice, casting their
head-gear into the flames, just as the people did
in the times of Romola.   We had started by
the Packet-boat from London Bridge, as I have
said, and immediately we came on board we
had been kindly greeted by a family group
already established there, an elderly gentleman
in clerical dress and a lady sitting with an
umbrella in the drizzle of rain and falling smuts
from the funnel.   This was the Kingsley family,
consisting of the Rector of Chelsea and his wife
and his two sons (Charles Kingsley was the
elder of the two), then going abroad for his
health.   It will now be seen that my recollections concern more historical head-dresses
than our unlucky bonnets; associations which
William Tell himself might not have disdained.
Mr. Kingsley and his brother were wearing
brown felt hats with very high and pointed
crowns, and with very broad brims, of a different
shape from my father's commonplace felt.
The hats worn by Mr. Kingsley and his brother

were more like those well-known brims and peaks which have crowned so many poets' heads since then.

It was a stormy crossing; the waves were curling unpleasantly round about the boat; I sat by Mrs. Kingsley, miserable, uncomfortable, and watching in a dazed and hypnotised sort of way the rim of Charles Kingsley's wide-awake as it rose and fell against the horrible horizon. He stood before us holding on to some ropes, and the horizon rose and fell, and the steamer pitched and tossed, and it seemed as if Time stood still.   But we reached those farther shores at last, and parted from our companions, and very soon afterwards my father told us with some amusement of the adventure which befell Mr. Charles Kingsley and his brother almost as soon as they landed, and after they had parted from their parents.   They were arrested by the police, who did not like the shape of their wide-awakes.   I may as well give the story in Mr. Kingsley's own words, which I found in his *Life* in an extract from a letter written immediately after the event to Mrs. Charles Kingsley at home :—

"'Here we are at Treves,' he says, 'having been brought there under arrest with a gendarme from the Mayor of Gettesburg, and liberated next morning with much laughter and many curses from the police here. However, we had the pleasure of spending a night in prison among fleas and felons, on the bare floor. The barbarians took our fishing-tackle for *Todt-instrumenten* and our wide-awakes for Italian hats, and got it into their addle-pates that we were emissaries of Mazzini. . . .'"

Perhaps I can find some excuse for the "addle-pates" when I remember that proud and eager head, and that bearing so full of character and energy. One can imagine the author of *Alton Locke* not finding very great favour with foreign mouchards and gendarmes, and suggesting indefinite terrors and suspicions to their minds.

Fortunately for the lovers of nature, unfortunately for autobiographers, the dates of the years as they pass are not written up in big letters on the blue vaults overhead, though the

seasons themselves are told in turn by the
clouds and lights and by every waving tree and
every country glade. And so, though one
remembers the aspect of things, the years are
apt to get a little shifted at times, and I cannot
quite tell whether it was this year or that one
following it, in which we found ourselves still
in glorious summer weather returning home
from distant places, and coming back by
Germany and by Weimar.

In common with most children, the stories
of our father's youth always delighted and
fascinated us, and we had often heard him
speak of his own early days at college and in
Germany, and of his happy stay at Pumper-
nickel-Weimar, where he went to Court and
saw the great Goethe, and was in love with the
beautiful Amalia von X. And now coming to
Weimar we found ourselves actually *alive* in
his past somehow, almost living it alongside
with him, just like Gogo in Mr. du Maurier's
story. I suddenly find myself walking up the
centre of an empty shady street, and my father
is pointing to a row of shutters on the first floor
of a large and comfortable-looking house,

"That is where Frau von X. used to live," he said. "How kind she was to us, and what a pretty girl Amalia was." And then a little further on we passed the house in the sunshine of a *plaz* in which he told us he himself had lodged with a friend; and then we came to the palace, with the soldiers and sentries looking like toys wound up from the Burlington Arcade, and going backwards and forwards with their spikes in front of their own striped boxes; and we saw the acacia trees with their cropped heads, and the iron gates; and we went across the courtyard into the palace and were shown the ball-room and the smaller saloons, and we stood on the shining floors and beheld the classic spot where for the first and only time in all his life, I believe, my father had invited the lovely Amalia to waltz. And then coming away all absorbed and delighted with our experiences in living backwards, my father suddenly said, "I wonder if old Weissenborne is still alive? He used to teach me German." And lo! as he spoke a tall, thin old man, in a broad-brimmed straw hat, with a beautiful Pomeranian poodle running before him, came stalking along with a newspaper under his arm. "Good gracious, that looks like—yes, that *is* Doctor Weissenborne. He is hardly changed a bit," said my father, stopping short for a moment, and then he too stepped forward quickly with an outstretched hand, and the old man in turn stopped, stared, frowned. "I am Thackeray, my name is Thackeray," said my father eagerly and shyly as was his way; and after another stare from the doctor, suddenly came a friendly lighting up and exclaiming and welcoming and handshaking and laughing, while the pretty white dog leapt up and down, as much interested as we were in the meeting.

"You have grown so gray I did not know you at first," said the doctor in English. And my father laughed, and said he was a great deal grayer now than the doctor himself; then he introduced us to the old man, who shook us gravely by the finger-tips with a certain austere friendliness, and once more turned again with a happy, kind, grim face to my father. Yes, he had followed his career with interest; he had heard of him from this man and that man; he had read one of his books,—not all.

Why had he never sent any ? why had he never come back before? "You must bring your misses and all come and breakfast at my lodging," said Dr. Weissenborne.

"And is this your old dog?" my father asked, after accepting the doctor's invitation. Dr. Weissenborne shook his head. Alas! the old dog was no more, he died two years before. Meanwhile the young dog was very much there, frisking and careering in cheerful circles round about us. The doctor and his dog had just been starting for their daily walk in the woods when they met us, and they now invited us to accompany them. We called at his lodging on the way to announce our return to breakfast, and then started off together for the park. The park (I am writing of years and years ago) was a bright green little wood, with leaves and twigs and cheerful lights, with small trees not very thickly planted on the steep slopes, with many narrow paths wandering into green depths, and with seats erected at intervals along the way. On one of these seats the old professor showed us an inscription cut deep into the wood with a knife, "*Doctor*

W. and his dog." Who had carved it? He
did not know.   But besides this inscription—on
every one of the benches where Goethe used
to rest, and on every tree which used to shade
his head—was written another inscription,
invisible indeed, and yet which we seemed to
read all along the way—" Here Goethe's life
was spent; here he walked, here he rested;
his feet have passed to and fro along this
narrow pathway."   The pathway led to his
garden-house.

It was lovely summer weather as I have
said, that weather which used to be so common
when one was young, and which I dare say our
children still discover now, though we cannot
always enjoy it.   We came back with our
friend the doctor and breakfasted with him in
his small apartment, in a room full of books, at
a tiny table drawn to an open window; then
after breakfast we sat in the Professor's garden
among the nasturtiums.   My sister and I were
given books to read ; they were translations
for the use of students, I remember; and the
old friends smoked together and talked over
a hundred things.   Amalia was married and

I

had several children : she was away. Madame von Goethe was still in Weimar with her sons, and Fräulein von Pogwishe, her sister, was also there. "They would be delighted to see you again," said the Professor. "We will go together, and leave the young misses here till our return." But not so; our father declared we also must be allowed to come. My recollections (according to the wont of such provoking things) here begin to fail me, and in the one particular which is of any interest; for though we visited Goethe's old house I can scarcely remember it at all, only that the doctor said Madame von Goethe had moved after Goethe's death. She lived in a handsome house in the town, with a fine staircase running up between straight walls, and leading into a sort of open hall, where, amid a good deal of marble and stateliness, stood two little unpretending ladies by a big round table piled with many books and papers. The ladies were Madame von Goethe and her sister. Doctor Weissenborne went first and announced an old friend, and then ensued more welcomings and friendly exclamations and quick recognitions on

both sides, all benevolently superintended by our
Virgil. "And are you both as fond of reading
novels as ever?" my father asked. The ladies
laughed. "Yes, indeed," they said, and pointed
to a boxful of books which had just arrived,
with several English novels among them, which
they had been unpacking as we came in. Then
the sons of the house were sent for,—kind and
friendly and unassuming young men, walking in,
and as much interested and pleased to witness
their parents' pleasure as we were; they were
not handsome, with nothing of their grandfather's noble aspect (as one sees it depicted),
but with most charming and courteous ways.
One was a painter, the mother told us, the other
a musician. And while my father talked to the
elder ladies, the young men took us younger
ones in hand. They offered to show us the
celebrated garden-house and asked us to drink
tea there next day. And so it happened that
once more we found ourselves being conducted
through the little shady wood. But to be
walking there with Goethe's family, with his
grandsons and their mother, the Ottilie who
had held the dying poet's hand to the last;

to be going to his favourite resort where so
much of his time was spent; to hear him so
familiarly quoted and spoken of was something
like hearing the distant echo of the great voice
itself: something like seeing the skirts of his
dressing-gown just waving before us.   And at
the age that I was then, impressions are so vivid
that I have always all my life had a vague
feeling of having been in Goethe's presence.
We seemed to find something of it everywhere,
most of all in the little garden-house, in the
bare and simple room where he used to write.
One of the kind young men went to the
window and showed us something on the pane.
What it was I know not clearly, but I think it
was the great name written with a diamond; and
finally in the garden, at a wooden table, among
trees and dancing shadows, we drank our tea,
and I remember Wolfgang von Goethe handing a tea-cup, and the look of it, and suddenly
the whole thing vanishes. . . . There was a
certain simple dignity and hospitality in it all
which seems to belong to all the traditions of
hospitable Weimar, and my father's pleasure
and happy emotion gave a value and import-

ance to every tiny detail of that short but happy time. Even the people at the inn remembered their old guest, and came to greet him; but also they sent in such an enormous bill as we were departing on the evening of the second day, that he exclaimed in dismay to the waiter, "So much for sentimental recollections! Tell the host I shall never be able to afford to come back to Weimar again."

The waiter stared; I wonder if he delivered the message. The hotel-bill I have just mentioned was a real disappointment to my father, and, alas for disillusions! another more serious shock, a meeting which was no meeting, somewhat dashed the remembrance of Amalia von X.

It happened at Venice, a year or two after our visit to Weimar. We were breakfasting at a long table where a fat lady also sat a little way off, with a pale fat little boy beside her. She was stout, she was dressed in light green, she was silent, she was eating an egg. The *sala* of the great marble hotel was shaded from the blaze of sunshine, but stray gleams shot across the dim hall, falling on the palms and

the orange trees beyond the lady, who gravely
shifted her place as the sunlight dazzled her.
Our own meal was also spread, and my sister
and I were only waiting for my father to begin.
He came in presently, saying he had been
looking at the guest-book in the outer hall, and
he had seen a name which had interested him
very much. "Frau von Z. Geboren von X.
It must be Amalia! She must be *here*—in the
hotel," he said; and as he spoke he asked a
waiter whether Madame von Z. was still in the
hotel. "I believe that is Madame von Z.,"
said the waiter, pointing to the fat lady. The
lady looked up and then went on with her egg,
and my poor father turned away, saying in a
low, overwhelmed voice, " *That* Amalia! That
cannot be Amalia." I could not understand
his silence, his discomposure. "Aren't you
going to speak to her? Oh, please do go and
speak to her!" we both cried. "Do make
sure if it is Amalia." But he shook his head.
"I can't," he said; "I had rather not."
Amalia meanwhile having finished her egg,
rose deliberately, put down her napkin and
walked away, followed by her little boy. . . .

Things don't happen altogether at the same
time; they don't quite begin or end all at once.
Once more I heard of Amalia long years afterwards, when by a happy hospitable chance I
met Dr. Norman Macleod at the house of my
old friends, Mr. and Mrs. Cunliffe. I was
looking at him, and thinking that in some
indefinable way he put me in mind of the past,
when he suddenly asked me if I knew that he
and my father had been together as boys at
Weimar, learning German from the same professor, and both in love with the same beautiful
girl. "What, Amalia? Dr. Weissenborne?"
I cried. "Dear me! do you know about
Amalia?" said Dr. Macleod, "and do you
know about old Weissenborne? I thought I
was the only person left to remember them.
We all learnt from Weissenborne; we were all
in love with Amalia, every one of us, your
father too! What happy days those were!"
And then he went on to tell us that years and
years afterwards, when they met again on the
occasion of one of the lecturing tours in Scotland, he, Dr. Macleod, and the rest of the
notabilities were all assembled to receive the

lecturer on the platform, and as my father came by carrying his papers and advancing to take his place at the reading-desk, he recognised Dr. Macleod as he passed, and in the face of all the audience he bent forward and said gravely, without stopping one moment on his way, "*Ich liebe Amalia doch*," and so went on to deliver his lecture.

Dr. Macleod also met Amalia once again in after life, and to him, too, had come a disillusion. He too had been overwhelmed and shocked by the change of years. Poor lady! I can't help being very sorry for her. To have had two such friends and not to have kept them seems a cruel fate. To have been so charming, that her present seemed but a calumny upon the past. It is like the story of the woman who flew into a fury with her own portrait, young, smiling, and triumphant, and who destroyed it, so as not to be taunted by the past any more. Let us hope that Frau von Z. was never conscious of her loss, never looked upon this picture and on that.

Since writing all this, I have found an old

letter from my father to his mother, and written from Weimar. It is dated 29th September 1830. "There is a capital library here," he says, "which is open to me, an excellent theatre which costs a shilling a night, and a charming *petite société* which costs nothing. Goethe, the great lion of Weimar, I have not yet seen, but his daughter-in-law has promised to introduce me." Then he describes going to Court : " I have had to air my legs in black breeches and to sport a black coat, black waistcoat, and cock-hat, looking something like a cross between a footman and a Methodist parson.

"We have had three operas," he goes on ; "*Medea* and the *Barber of Seville* and the *Flauto Magico*. Hümmel conducts the orchestra [then comes a sketch of Hümmel with huge shirt collars]. The orchestra is excellent, but the singers are not first-rate." . . . Amalia must have had rivals, even in those early days, for this same letter goes on to say : " I have fallen in love with the Princess of Weimar, who is unluckily married to Prince Charles of Prussia. I must get over this unfortunate passion, which will otherwise, I fear, bring me to an untimely end. There are several very charming young persons of the female sex here; Miss Amalia von X. and ditto von Pappenheim are the evening belles."

"Of winter nights," says my father in the other well-known letter which is printed in Lewes's *Life of Goethe*, "we used to charter sedan chairs, in which we were carried through the snow to those pleasant Court entertainments. I for my part was fortunate enough to purchase Schiller's sword, which formed a part of my Court costume and still hangs in my study,[1] and puts me in mind of days of youth the most kindly and delightful."

---

[1] So he wrote in 1855, but a few years after he gave the sword to a friend for whom he had a great affection, who carried it back to America as a token of good will and sympathy. This friend was Bayard Taylor, a true knight, and worthy to carry the honourable bloodless weapon.

CHAPTER IX

ONE day Jackson drove the blue fly up to the door, and my father, looking rather smart, with a packet of papers in his hand, and my grandmother who had come over from Paris, and my sister and I all got in, and we drove away, a nervous company, to Willis's Rooms to hear the first of the lectures upon the English Humorists. My father was of course very nervous, but as we drove along he made little jokes to reassure us all; then together we mounted the carpeted staircase leading to the long empty room, and after a time he left us. I have no very pleasant recollection of that particular half-hour of my life. I remember the unoccupied chairs, and people coming in rather subdued, as if into a church. Many of the windows were open, the sky looked very blue over the roof-tops, our hearts were thumping, the carriages outside came driving up, with distant rumbling sounds, growing louder and louder; and I remember wondering at the time whether I should mind very much if the day of judgment could suddenly come upon us and thus put an end to this terrible ordeal, which desperate imagination was a real consolation to me at the moment.   It is a happiness to realise now who it was who came to my dear father's help when all our emotion and sympathy was, I fear, only a hindrance.   I cannot help giving the passage out of Mrs. Kemble's records concerning my father's lectures, although it may have already been quoted by others.

I met Thackeray at Miss Perry's at dinner, a few days before he began his course of lectures on the English Essayists, and he asked me to come and hear him, and told me he was so nervous about it, that he was afraid he should break down. . . .

He was to lecture at Willis's Rooms, in the same room where I read; and going thither before the time for his beginning, I found him standing like a forlorn, disconsolate giant in the middle of the room, gazing about him.   "Oh Lord," he exclaimed, as he shook hands with me, "I'm sick at my stomach with fright!"   I spoke some words of encouragement to him, and was going away, but he held my hand like a scared child, crying, "Oh, don't leave me!" "But," said I, "Thackeray, you mustn't stand here. Your audience are beginning to come in"; and I drew him from the middle of the chairs and benches, which were beginning to be occupied, into the retiring-room adjoining the lecture-room, my own reading having made me perfectly familiar with both. "Oh," he said, "if I could only get at that confounded thing [his lecture], to have a last look at it!" "Where is it?" said I. "Oh, in the next room on the reading-desk." "Well," said I, "if you don't like to go in and get it, I'll fetch it for you." And remembering well the position of my reading-table, which had been close to the door of the retiring-room, I darted in, hoping to snatch the manuscript without attracting the attention of the audience, with which the room was already nearly full. I had been used to deliver my readings seated, at a very low table, but my friend Thackeray gave his lectures standing, and had had a reading-desk placed on the platform, adapted to his own very tall stature, so that when I came to get his manuscript it was almost above my head. Though rather disconcerted, I was determined not to go back without it, and so made a half jump and a clutch at the book, when every leaf of it (they were not fastened together) came fluttering separately down about me. I hardly know what I did, but I think I must have gone nearly on all fours in my agony to gather up the scattered leaves, and retreating with them, held them out in dismay to poor Thackeray crying, "Oh, look, look what a dreadful thing I have done!" "My dear soul," said he, "you couldn't have done better, for me. I have just a quarter of an hour to wait here, and it will take me about that to page this again, and it's the best thing in the world that could have happened."

And meanwhile my father was paging the manuscript, and we were waiting outside, and the people kept coming in more and more quickly and filling up the places in front of us, behind us, all round us, settling down, unfastening their wraps, nodding to each other. I was gazing at a lady who had taken off her bonnet · and sat in a little Quaker cap just in front of me, when suddenly, there stood my father facing this great roomful. Though we had been waiting all the time, he came sooner than we expected. His voice sounded strained and odd for an instant, and I didn't recognise it. " In treating of the English humorists of the eighteenth century, it is of the men rather than of their works," so the strange voice began, and then almost immediately it softened and deepened and became his own : and at the same time as he stood there I realised that he looked just like himself; there was his waistcoat and his watch-chain, and my vague youthful spinnings, and chokings, began to subside.

I was now glad the day of judgment hadn't come. I don't remember taking in one word after the first sentence, but sat staring and

taking breath, and realising somehow that all
was going well. Among other things I did
notice, and do remember, the proud and happy
look of light and relief in my grandmother's
face, and her beautiful gray eyes all shining
when the people applauded and the lecture was
over just as unexpectedly as it had begun,
and the lady in the Quaker cap tied her
bonnet on again, — somebody said she was
the Duchess of Sutherland,—the people were
all talking and crowding up and shaking hands
with the lecturer. Then came the happy drive
home; Jackson made the horse gallop, and my
father laughed and made real jokes, without
any effort, and we laughed and enjoyed every
jolt and turning, on the way home.

These lectures gradually became a part of
our everyday life, just as much as the books
and the articles my father used to write, for
the little printers' boys waiting and swinging
their legs in the hall. Young Men's Institutes
and provincial agencies used to invite him
to the north and to the south. He came
and he went; sometimes he read in the
suburbs or at friends' houses, at Mrs. Procter's

and elsewhere; once he read at home, at the request, I think, of his well-loved Mrs. Elliot and Miss Perry. Sometimes he took us with him when he was not going very far from home. To this day I can enjoy that glorious summer's day we first spent at Oxford among the gardens and the gables, and where, with our host, St. John Thackeray, we stood in the street outside watching the backs of the audience pressing in to hear the lecture.

One year my father told us that he was going away—he was going to America to give his lectures there; he was going as soon as he had finished the book upon which he was engaged, and we were to spend the winter in Paris during his absence. " I must replace my patrimony," he said, " and make some provision for your mother and for you, and you must go to my mother's and spend the winter with her; you must work as hard as you can while I am away, and consider yourselves at college in a fashion, and learn French and a little music to play me to sleep of an evening when I come home." Alas! we neither of us could ever make enough music to send him to sleep, though I have often sent him out of the room. My hair used to stand on end, my fingers used to turn to stone when I tried to play to him ; even the things I liked best seemed to go off the rails in some general catastrophe.

America was farther away then than it is now, when a thousand Columbuses or Columbi (whatever the plural may be) cross the ocean week by week with a parting nod and a return ticket. That whole summer of 1854 seemed darkened by the coming separation. It was a long and burning summer ; even the shadows seemed burnt up, and so were the gardens at the back of the houses, and the brown turf and the avenues of Kensington Gardens, those gardens where that strange mist which is not quite fog nor quite real, nor even a fancy, but which has always seemed to me to be the very spirit of London itself, comes rising along the straight and formal distances. My father was hard at work finishing a book which some people still say is the best of all his books. People read it then, when it came out, and read it still and re-read it. He used to write in his study with the vine shading the two windows,

K

and we used to do our lessons, or sit sewing
and reading in the front room with the bow-
window to the street; and one day, as we were
there with our governess, my father came in, in
great excitement. "There's a young fellow
just come," said he; "he has brought a thousand
pounds in his pocket; he has made me an offer
for my book, it's the most spirited, handsome
offer, I scarcely like to take him at his word;
he's hardly more than a boy, his name is George
Smith; he is waiting there now, and I must go
back"; and then, after walking once up and
down the room, my father went away, and for
the first time, a life-time ago, I heard the name
of this good friend-to-be.

A great many arrangements were made for
the coming year's absence; there was a talk of
letting the house, but it was only shut up with
a couple of old servants to keep it. My father's
servants rarely left him. His old publishers
gave him a silver punch-bowl, and his new
publisher (I am writing of nearly half a century
ago) gave him a beautiful despatch-box; and
this same good friend gave to my sister and to
me a noble drawing of our father's head by

Samuel Lawrence that we might look at while
he was away. Then we all set off and went
abroad to rejoin our grandmother and grandfather, and for a little while we travelled together,
and then my father had to leave us. I can see
him now as he stood beside a wooden column at
some railway junction, Olten, I think it was, and
he stooped to kiss us ; and then he put us into
our railway carriage, and we were carried off with
heavy hearts while he stood looking at us fixedly,
tall and straight, and the train scudded off.
Somehow we never got used to these partings,
though our father returned each time safe and
in good spirits, and pleased with his journey
and its results. . . .

People can still walk through Kensington
Square and look up at the house yet standing
with its windows facing westward, in which
Rachel Castlewood once dwelt, and where
Colonel Esmond came, and where the Pretender
also came in his blonde periwig and blue ribbon,
and threw away—so Colonel Esmond tells us
—a kingdom for a passing fancy. In so looking they may well people the past with figures
all touched with its colour, and yet so strangely

living still, that as one reads one seems to have
known them all.   But any one who should try
to follow the familiar shades out of the precincts
of Kensington Square, and beyond Young Street,
where the porters with the chairs must have
passed, into the high road beyond which leads to
London, must be imaginative indeed to conjure
up their remembrance any more.   The *King's
Arms*, where the conspirators were assembled
when King George was proclaimed, has vanished out of sight; its quiet gardens are piled
up high with bricks and stories rearing like a
new Babel to the sky.   There are cities spreading where the market-gardens were flowering
but yesterday, tram-cars passing, engines whist-
ling.   I can scarcely imagine my father himself
writing *Esmond* in such a chaos.   Novels of
the future will take place by telegram, in flats,
in lifts, in metropolitan railways—they will
whirl Ixion-like on perpetual bicycles and
wheels.   It is difficult to imagine devotion such
as Esmond's continuing in this present sequence
of events; it seems as if new impulses, both
physical and mental, must arise in such a multi-
plicity of impressions; as if a new race must

people the earth. Beatrix indeed might belong to these later times; but Esmond and
Lady Castlewood would seem strangely out of
place.

Some one not long ago gave me a little map
of Kensington in 1764 by which one can see
what lanes and green fields and gardens then
lay between the village and London, more than
a mile away. Nursery gardens, wide open
spaces, brick kilns on Campden Hill and Gravel
Pits. In the midst of green fields stood three
or four houses called Bays Watering. The Serpentine was called the New River, Kensington
Gore consisted of five houses; Hogmore Lane
and Lobb's Field ran from the high road towards Chelsea. It is easier to imagine something than nothing at all, though I have the
map before me I can hardly feel that it is
true, and yet I remember Hogmore Lane, and
there was Love Lane just beyond, along which
we used to go for straggling walks on early
summer mornings with our playfellows, the
Coles, who lived in the terrace close by. We
used to start about six o'clock and bring home
branches of hawthorn blossom to decorate our

school-rooms and to remind us that it was May time.

There is one part of London which however still seems to me little changed, and this is Cheyne Row, which used to be at the end of all these hawthorn lanes, and Chelsea, whither we used often to go as children, crossing these lanes and fields, and coming by a pond and a narrow street called Paradise Row into the King's Road, and then after a few minutes' walk to Cheyne Row, where Mr. and Mrs. Carlyle lived to the end of their lives, and which seems to all of us made living still by their dead footsteps.

The old house in Cheyne Row is one of the first things I can remember when we came to London. Its stillness, its dimness, its panelled walls, its carved banisters, and the quiet garden behind, where at intervals in the brickwork lay the tobacco-pipes all ready for use; little Nero, the doggie, in his little coat, barking and trembling in every limb—it all comes before one with so much clearness, that, although so much has been said about that home, I cannot omit all mention of a place which made so vivid a part of my early life.

In the dining-room stood that enchanting
screen covered with pictures, drawings, prints,
fashions, portraits without end, which my father
liked so much; upstairs was the panelled
drawing-room with its windows to the Row,
and the portrait of Oliver Cromwell hanging
opposite the windows. But best of all, there
was Mrs. Carlyle herself, a living picture;
Gainsborough should have been alive to paint
her; slim, bright, dark-eyed, upright, in her place.
She looked like one of the grand ladies our
father used sometimes to take us to call upon.
She used to be handsomely dressed in velvet
and point lace. She sat there at leisure, and
prepared for conversation. She was not familiar,
but cordial, dignified, and interested in everything as she sat installed in her corner of the
sofa by one of the little tables covered with
nicknacks of silver and mother-of-pearl.

Almost the first time we ever went to see
her we had walked to Chelsea through the
snow, and across those lanes which have now
become South Kensington, and when we arrived,
numb and chilled and tired, we found in the
dining-room below, standing before the fire,

two delicious hot cups of chocolate all ready
prepared for us, with saucers placed upon the
top. " I thought ye would be frozen," said she ;
and the hot chocolate became a sort of institu-
tion.   Again and again she has sat by, benevolent and spirited, superintending our wintry
feasts, inviting our confidences, confiding in us
to a certain degree.

She used to tell us many of the stories which
have since come into print.   She was never
weary of discoursing of " Carlyle," of his genius,
his dyspepsia, of quoting his sayings.   " If you
wish for a quiet life," she used to say, " never
you marry a dyspeptic man of genius."   I remember she used to tell us, when he first grew
a beard, how all the time he had saved by
ceasing to shave he spent wandering about the
house, and bemoaning that which was amiss in
the universe.   As children we did not have
much of Carlyle's company ; if he came in and
sat down in the arm-chair, which was his, on the
opposite side to the sofa, we immediately went
away ; but the sense of his presence overhead
in the study distinctly added to our enjoyment
so long as he remained upstairs.   Mrs. Carlyle

used to tell us of her early life, of her passion
for study. Many of her admonitions and
friendly warnings have remained in my memory.
Once, looking expressively at me with her dark
eyes, she began to speak of self-control. "We
have all," she said, "a great deal more power
over our minds than it is at all the fashion to
allow, and an infinity of resource and ability to
use it. There was a time in my own life," she
said, "when I felt that unless I strove against
the feeling with all my strength and might I
should be crazed outright. I passed through
that time safely ; I was able to fight it out and
not to let myself go. People *can* help themselves, that I am convinced of, and that fact is
not nearly enough dwelt upon."

One day we went there ; we were no longer
children. I was a grown young lady, keeping
a diary at the time, in which I find the
following record of a brown paper parcel :—
"To Mrs. Carlyle's, where we found Lady
Stanley of Alderley just leaving the room ;
then Mrs. Carlyle, taking up the talk
again, immediately began speaking enthusias-
tically about *Adam Bede*. She had written to

the author, she said ; she had received grateful
messages from him in reply. She said that
Mr. Carlyle quite declined reading the book,
and when she expressed a hope that it might
be sent to her, 'What should he send it to *you*
for?' he said. 'Why shouldn't he send it?'
she answered ; 'he sent me the other.' 'You
are just like all weemen,' said he. (Mrs.
Carlyle always says weemen.)   'You are
always forming unreasonable expectations.'"

"We were going away, for we heard a
ring at the bell, which seemed to betoken fresh
visitors.   Then the door opened, and in came,
not visitors, but Charly the maid, carrying an
unmistakable publisher's brown-paper parcel.
Mr. Carlyle, who had followed her in, came
and sat down upon the sofa. Mrs. Carlyle
exclaimed and started forward. We opened
our eyes in delighted partisanship ; the string
was cut, and there sure enough were the three
orange volumes of *Adam Bede* sent with the
author's compliments. . . ."

Here are two notes addressed to my father
in the philosopher's cramped handwriting :—

CHELSEA, 24*th May* 1860.[1]

Alas, dear Thackeray, I durst as soon undertake to dance a hornpipe on the top of Bond Steeple, as to eat a white-bait dinner in my present low and lost state! Never in my life was I at such a pass. You are a good brother man; and I am grateful. Pray for me, and still hope for me if you can.—Yours ever,   T. CARLYLE.

CHELSEA, 26*th May* 1860.

DEAR THACKERAY,—The thing I contemplated just now (or the nucleus of the thing) was a letter concerning that anecdote about *Fontenoy.* "*Faites feu, Messieurs,*" on the part of the English, with answer from the *Gardes Françaises,* "Begin you, gentlemen; wouldn't do such a thing for the world!" My letter is from Lord Charles Hay, Captain of the Scots Fusiliers, main actor in the business; it was sent me last year by Lord Gifford; and I could have made a little story out of it which would have been worth publishing.

But on applying to Lord Gifford, he (what he is himself, I believe, truly sorry for) cannot at present give me permission. So the poor little enterprise falls to nothing again; and I may be said to be in a state of ill-luck just now!

If I ever in the end of this book have life left, you shall have plenty of things. But for the time being I can only answer *de profundis* to the above effect.

Fair wind and full sea to you in this hitherto so successful voyage, for which the omens certainly are on all sides good. Your people do not send me a copy (since No. I.); but we always draw our purse upon it to the small extent requisite.—Yours ever truly,   T. CARLYLE.

---

[1] These notes were written when the *Cornhill* was first started, an eventful time in our lives.

Some voices are those which speak to us; others speak for us. The first belong to the immortals who dwell apart somewhere beyond the boundaries of common life and moods, and it is, perhaps, for that very reason they are best able to give utterance to oracles; the others belong to humanity itself, and among these latter voices, who would not reckon Carlyle's? . . .

"I wish you could get Carlyle's miscellaneous criticisms," wrote my father in 1839, in a letter to his mother. "I have read a little in the book. A nobler one does not live in our language, I am sure, and one that will have such an effect on our ways of thought and prejudices. Criticism has been a party matter with us till now, and literature is a poor political lacquey. Please God we shall begin, ere long, to love art for art's sake. It is Carlyle who has worked more than any other to give it its independence."

I went out with my father one evening in the winter of 1863, and as we were driving along in the dusk by the Serpentine we passed Carlyle walking across the park, and my father seeing him, leant forward and waved his hands. "A great benevolent shower of salutations," Carlyle called it, when he spoke in after days of this last meeting.

After Mrs. Carlyle's death, it was Mr. Carlyle that we used to go and see in her old drawing-room, which he now took to inhabiting altogether. It was no surprise, when his history was told, to realise that he had been constantly cross and often contrary ; but that passion of tender love and remorse and devotion came as a revelation, all the more moving that one had almost guessed it at times. It was when my own father died that something was revealed to us of that deep and tender feeling.

It will be remembered that in Lewes's *Life of Goethe* there is an account of a birthday gift sent by fifteen Englishmen to Goethe. "The young Carlyle who had been cheered through his struggling sadness and strengthened for the part he was to play in life, by the beauty and the wisdom which Goethe had revealed to him, conceived the idea that it would be a pleasant and fitting thing if some of the few admirers of Goethe in England forwarded to Weimar a trifling token of their admiration.   On reaching home Mrs. Carlyle at once sketched the design of a seal to be engraved—the Serpent of Eternity encircling a star, with the words "Ohne Hast Ohne Rast" (unhasting, unresting), in allusion to the well-known verses—

> " Like a Star, unhasting unresting,
> Be each one fulfilling his God-given hest."

Long years afterwards another small presentation took place to Carlyle himself, at a time when he was living in Cheyne Row with his niece. There had been some alarm of housebreakers in Chelsea, which sacrilegious housebreakers, not content with robbing ordinary people, broke into Mr. Carlyle's house and ran away again, without carrying off anything more valuable than the dining-room clock.   As I have said, it was the remembrance of this little incident of the seal which suggested to some one the idea of replacing the stolen clock, and about fifteen of Carlyle's friends and admirers subscribed to purchase one, a small sign of their respect and goodwill.   Among these were his old friends Lady Stanley of Alderley, the Countess of Airlie, and Mrs. Oliphant.   Lady Stanley was asked to be spokeswoman on the occasion, and to present the gift. It was Carlyle's birthday, and a dismal winter's day,[1] the streets were shrouded in greenish vapours, and the houses looked no less more dreary within, than the streets through which we had come. Somewhat chilled and depressed, we all assembled in Lady Stanley's great drawing-room in Dover Street, where the fog had also penetrated, and presently from the further end of the room, advancing through shifting darkness, came Carlyle. There was a moment's pause. No one moved ; he stood in the middle of the room without speaking. No doubt the philosopher, as well as his disciples, felt the influence of the atmosphere. Lady Stanley went to meet him. "Here is a little birthday present we want you to accept from us all, Mr. Carlyle," said she, quickly pushing up before him a small table, upon which stood the clock ticking all ready for his acceptance. Then came another silence, broken by a knell sadly sounding in our ears. "Eh, what have I got to do with Time any more?" he said. It was a melancholy moment.

---

[1] Carlyle was born December 4, 1794.

Nobody could speak.   The unfortunate pro-
moter of the scheme felt her heart sinking into
her shoes.   Had she but had the wit to answer
him cheerfully, to assure him that anyhow time
had a great deal to do with him, the little
ceremony might have been less of a fiasco than
it assuredly was; and yet I think afterwards
the old man must have been pleased, and liked
to think that he was remembered.   Few people
could value sincerity as he did, or better know
the worth of love and affectionate respect.

After Carlyle himself was laid to rest I went
for the last time to look at the house, which I
remembered all my life; my little boy was with
me, and he began crowing and pointing to the
old screen full of pictures, some of which his
grandfather had drawn.   The screen still stood
in its place in the dining-room.   From behind
the old screen came Mrs. Alexander Carlyle,
carrying her little Tom, who, seeing a fellow-
baby, uttered three deep notes of interest, and
in them was some strange echo of the familiar
voice that had filled the house so long, and
reached how far beyond its walls!

CHAPTER X

I HAVE already mentioned my father's tour in America when he went to deliver those lectures which had been so successful in England. Saying good-bye is the price one has to pay even for a prosperous and fortunate expedition. I can still see him as he stood on the platform of the railway-station at Olten, in Belgium, where we parted. He stood by a slender iron column, looking very tall and very sad as he watched the train go off in which we were bound for Switzerland with our grandparents. He himself was returning to England through Germany. He had to correct the proofs of *Esmond* before he left, and to give some more lectures in the provinces, and to wind up things at home.

L

My grandmother was very miserable and nervous. She had brought him a life-belt for his cabin as a farewell gift, and thoroughly frightened herself by so doing. We were too young to be nervous, but we were very unhappy. Our dear old grandfather did his best to cheer us all, and after we had parted from my father he made out all sorts of pleasant little plans, and ordered various special *compotes* and tartlets at the hotels suited to our youthful appetites. He took us for walks and to visit museums, and he always consulted any fellow-travellers and sight-seers as to our next movements. Indeed our journeyings greatly depended upon these chance encounters and recommendations. The first night, when we put up at some little inn, the waiter brought us the travellers' book to write our names in ; I forget all about the place, but I can see the book and the table spread, and what I do most vividly remember is our despair when, instead of the neat *Mr. Thackeray and family* to which we were used, we read the following announcement in our grandfather's handwriting : *Schmid Major, en retraite, avec Madame sa épouse et ses deux*

Mademoiselles. My grandmother, sad as she was, began to laugh, and we all entreated our dear old Major to make some changes in the inscription, but he stuck to it, and would not alter a single letter.

We reached Geneva after some days. There at the *poste restante* we found various letters waiting, and news of our father. "As for the arrival at this place [he was writing from Salzburg], it's like entering into fairyland, it is so beautiful; and the Tyrol is delightful too, but not like our Switzerland. And one Swiss cottage is uncommonly like another, and with five or six days of rocks and pine-woods I feel somehow as if I've had enough!" Then a little further on he writes: "Give my love to my dearest mother, and have her to understand that this blew devil of which I complain is only an artistic blew devil, and that he comes always before I get to work, and that there is no other reason. . . . There is bad music here for a wonder at the beer-garden; though I amused myself very well there yesterday, opposite a pretty little child of three years, who ate three sausages with her fingers and without any bread, all except a little bit which she gave out of her mouth to her mamma. And I went up a hill to a Capuchin convent and saw some of my favourite dirty scoundrels with beards, and the town clinks all over with Austrian sabres."

I never think of Geneva and of those particular days without a curious feeling of terror and emotion. We were in a tall hotel with windows looking towards the lake, and it was lovely summer weather, but it was a dismal time. My dear grandmother sought for sympathy among the people to whom she was naturally drawn, the masters and teachers belonging to the Protestant Church in Geneva. They were interesting and important personages, who inspired me with a curious mixture of respect and discomfort, and to whom my grandmother had brought various introductions from her friends the French Protestant *pasteurs* at Paris.

There was a garden to which she took me, not far from our hotel, with beautiful shady trees and spreading grass. In the garden stood a white chapel, clean, light, bare, decorous, with some black and white marble ornamentations.

A woman in a black frilled cap showed us to our seats, and there we waited, listening for some time to a clanging bell. Then the service began. Only one or two people came to it, but the place, although to others it might speak of most fervent and passionate emotion, seemed oppressive with chill and silent religion to me. When all was over, my grandmother had some low-voiced conversation with the woman in the black cap, who beckoned to the bell-ringer, and the result of the whispering was that, after a short delay, we were led across the grass and under the trees to a retired part of the garden, where in the shade of some bushes sat an old man of very noble aspect, with long white hair falling on his shoulders. He looked to me like some superior being. Indeed, to my excited imagination it seemed as if I was being brought up to the feet of a prophet, to some inspired person who was sitting there in authority and in judgment on all the rest of the world. This old man was M. César Malan, the head of a section of the Calvinist Church in Geneva, whose name was well known and very widely respected. He had built the chapel in his

garden. Not a little to my consternation, after
a few words with my grandmother, he immediately, with the utmost kindness, began asking
me questions about myself, about my convictions, my religious impressions, my hopes, my
future aspirations. He was very kind, but even
an angel from heaven would be alarming,
suddenly appearing to a girl of fifteen with such
a catechism. The more kindly he pressed me,
the less able I was to answer. Sometimes I
said too much, sometimes I was hopelessly
silent, and in the midst of a nervous discussion
as to the ultimate fate of Judas (I felt somewhat akin to him myself) the scene ended in
my bursting into tears of embarrassment and
hopeless confusion. I was consoled on our
return to the hotel by my grandfather, who was
most sympathetic. "Those, my dear child,"
he said, "who have studied deeply, who are
able to read the Scriptures in the original, are
far more likely than you or I to be able to judge
correctly upon such important subjects, and we
had therefore better leave all such speculations
entirely to them."

That next winter, which we spent in Paris,

we used to attend the classes of a man even better known than César Malan, Adolphe Monod, who remains to me one of the most striking and noble figures I have ever met; his face, his dark eyes, all spoke as well as his eloquent voice, and above all his earnest life and ways. To me he seemed the St. Paul of my own time; and those classes which cost so many tears, and which gave rise to so much agitated discussion, are still among the most touching and heart-reaching experiences of my life. I can see the girls' faces now, as they listened to their beloved *pasteur*. Our hearts were in our lessons, as his was in his teaching, undoubtedly; we were all in earnest and ready to follow; only, though I longed to be convinced, I could only admire and love the lesson and the teacher as well. He warned, encouraged, explained in his earnest, gentle voice. "Ah, mes enfants," I can hear him saying, "fuyez, fuyez ce monde!" Fly the world! If ever the world was delightful and full of interest it was then—the daily task, the hour and its incidents eventful and absorbing; if ever our hearts were open to receive, not to reject it, it was then.

M. Monod himself was no unimportant factor
in my world. I once saw Faraday, who re-
minded me of him. M. Monod only once came
to our house to see my grandmother, and I met
him on the staircase, but he passed me by, and
did not recognise me out of my place in the
second row of chairs, nor did I venture to speak
to him. I still remember the strange thrill we
felt, and which ran in a whisper along the class,
when we heard that Henrietta P. had been
refused her first communion for going to a ball
within a week of the event. She came no more
to the meetings. The girls sat in their places
on rows of straw chairs, and many of the parents
accompanied them. Sometimes in a corner by
the window holding up a small Bible, in which
he followed the references with attention, there
sat an oldish gentleman, who was (so we were
told) the great Prime Minister, M. Guizot.

My father did not sail for America till the
autumn of that year, but we remained on
at Paris with our grandparents. The sun
streamed into our apartment all day long, for
we had windows looking to every side of the

compass. When Paris was getting intolerably hot, we started for the country, where my grandfather had taken a country house on a lease for two or three years, in a village called Mennecy, near Corbeil. Mennecy was a straggling little village among peat fields, crossed by narrow black streams, or canals, of the colour of the peat. Growing by the banks were long rows of stumpy willow trees, cut year by year for the sake of the osiers, which were sold to the basket-makers. Here and there, perhaps at the turn of the stream, some single tree had been allowed to grow to its natural dimensions, forming a sequestered nook where some of us used to bathe on hot summer days. Two young friends of my grandmother's, Laura and Pauline C., were with us most of the time we were living in this *villeggiatura*, and Pauline especially loved the water, and used to come home fresh and smiling and pluming herself after her cool divings. Mennecy was a rural quiet spot among willow trees, and a perfect retreat in hot summer weather.

There was an old paved *place* in the centre

of the village, leading to a fine old church well
served and well frequented, of which the
Sunday bells clanged far across the country.
We used to see the congregation assembling
in cheerful companies, arriving from outlying
farms, and greeting each other in the market-
place before the Mass began ; a congregation
with more of talk and animation than with us,
with blue smocks and white linen *coiffes* and
picturesque country cloaks and *sabots*. We
used somewhat ruefully to wish to follow
Pauline and Louise (our cross maid-of-all-work)
through the swing doors behind which the
incense was tossing and the organ rolling out
its triumphant fugue. A Roman Catholic
service seems something of a high festival,
coming round Sunday after Sunday, bringing
excitement and adoration along with it. Our
own village church-bells also ring out, calling
to the peaceful congregations ; calling us to
something more tranquil, more free, more full
of individual feeling, but it is an aspiration
rather than a rite.

My grandparents' house had once been a
hunting-lodge belonging to Henry the Fourth,

who loved the neighbourhood and frequented
Compiègne long years before the President
Louis Napoleon, or the Emperor Napoleon
the Third, and his courtiers, and their ladies
in hunting costumes, and with spirited horses
and *fanfarons*, all followed the chase. I don't
remember ever seeing any of them, but we
had a general impression that these hunting
companies were about, and any day a gay
procession, not unlike something out of a fairy
tale, might come riding past our old gates.
They were old creaking gates which had once
been green, now gray and weather-stained;
our high walls, which had once been white,
were also green and stained and overgrown by
a vine. M. Roche had given us *Jocelin* to
read about a year before, and I used to think
of the description of the *curé's* home as I stood
in the old courtyard at Mennecy, with its well
and its vine-clad walls. There was an old well
with a wrought-iron top to it and a rope, and
there was a vine travelling along the margin
and spreading beyond it, along the wrought-
iron railing, to the pretty old iron gate dividing
the courtyard from the old garden at the back,

which with its dainty rusty iron scrolls excluded the cocks and hens, that flapped and picketed and strutted all day long in the front court, and roosted at night in the great empty stables opposite our house.

The hunting-lodge before it had become our home had been turned into a farm; the knights and cavaliers had made way for blouses and cowherds, and the hunters had given up their stalls to heavy cart-horses, though indeed there was room to spare for any number of either. But the farmer died in time and his widow married the milkman, and she let the old place to my grandfather, who had a special purpose in coming to Mennecy.

A flight of stone steps led from the court-yard to the house, just as one sees in Scotland, which looks so like France in places. Our front windows opened on to a garden, and the passages and the sitting-rooms were panelled in some parts. We could walk all round the drawing-room between the panels and the walls; nor was it dark within the wainscot, for there were two little windows at either end to give light to the spiders and the active mice

who chiefly frequented this passage. The
floors were all of brick, on which we had laid
a carpet, and my grandmother had brought a
blue sofa and chairs from Paris, and hired a
piano in Corbeil.

"Quel charmant meuble!" our neighbour
the Maire used to say when he came in of an
evening, bowing politely to the piano and then
to us. Polished rosewood! ivory keys! gilt
handles! he was genuine in his enthusiastic
admiration. To hear him, one would think
there had never been such a piano since the
world began. It got very much out of tune,
but that did not shake our faith in it. We
gave parties on the strength of the *charmant
meuble*. Piano-company (so we considered
ourselves) was not so very common in the
neighbourhood. Laura could play (as she still
does) to the delight of her listeners; Pauline
had a very sweet voice, and used to sing to the
piano and to us of summer evenings. M. le
Maire was also very fond of singing and of
being accompanied. His wife was not musical,
but our young ladies were very patient and
kind, and used to repeat the more difficult

passages over and over again for him, and try
not to laugh when he went very much out
of tune. My sister and I used to find the
panelled passages a convenient retreat occasionally, when a note went very wildly astray ;
or we could always run out through the French
windows into the garden, where the grass-
hoppers' concert would also strike up of fine
summer evenings, and seemed to whistle and
spread far, far beyond the corn-fields and the
poppy-heads. There was a terrace at the end
of the garden, where a pavilion stood, over-
looking the high road, from which we could
see the regiments as they passed on their way
to Corbeil, and the dragoons watering their
horses at the little village inn. All along this
terrace grew pumpkin plants, which we scarcely
noticed when we first arrived, although we
were full of admiration for the luxuriant vines
hanging from all the walls, and of which one
charming tunnelled avenue ran right across a
corner of the garden. Pauline and I used to
sit there that summer time under the green
shadows, making believe to learn Italian with
Goldoni and a dictionary. That is to say, I

was making believe; she not only learned the language, but married a Milanese gentleman in after years. Only the other day, as we sat entranced by Madame Dusé's gracious inspirations, I seemed for the first time to enter into the real spirit of those bygone and almost forgotten studies. Goldoni suddenly came to life again, and I thought of the old green vine avenue, and the books I had been bored by as a girl began to speak to me for the first time. As the autumn went on, myriads of wasps appeared; the grapes swelled and turned to golden sweetness; we used to go into the garden with hunches of bread, and gather our own breakfasts and luncheons growing on the walls. Along with the grapes came the pumpkins, and they also grew. Cinderella's were nothing to them; the huge balls came swelling and rolling down upon us, colouring and rising in every direction. We got frightened at last, it seemed wicked to waste them; we boiled them, we passed them through sieves, we steeped them in milk by the Maire's advice. At the end of three or four days we absolutely loathed them. The pigs of the neighbourhood, already satiated with pumpkin, refused to touch them any more. On the fifth day a neighbour sent us in a great basketful as a present. We were literally bombarded with pumpkins that year, but let us hope it was a specially good year for fruit.

I said that my grandfather had a special purpose in view when he brought us to Mennecy. Our dear Colonel Newcome had a fancy that he could rehabilitate the family fortunes by establishing a manufactory for peat fuel, which was to be made by the help of a certain machine. It had been invented by an old friend, who had sold him the patent for a certain sum and as a special favour. This same friend, who seems to have been an ingenious, though an expensive acquaintance, had also invented a wooden horse which was to supersede the usual living quadrupeds. It had the great advantage of only eating coal and coke, but I believe it was found all the same to be much more expensive than the real animal, and far less intelligent. I remember seeing the elaborately carved hoofs of the wooden horse standing on the piano, with a drawing of his cast-iron inside. I was only once shown the peat-machine ; it looked something like a stove, and used to be poked by an old woman, while a little boy with a barrow brought up the peat, which was then and there turned into black cakes. We never made our fortunes out of the peat, but we burnt a great stack of it, which glowed bright and clear and lasted through several winters, and I believe the whole thing was finally handed over to an experimentalist on the spot, who may still be there, for all I know. He was a short and swarthy man, who used to come and bargain in the dining-room at enormous length.

As my grandparents had spent several summers at Mennecy they had made acquaintance with the two or three neighbours, and with the family at the _château_. We used to pass the _château_ when we walked along the high road, which was divided from the park by a wall. Here and there were iron gates through which we could see into the shady avenues of poplar trees and nut trees, and in one place, where an old bridge crossed a stream, we caught sight of the old white house with its shutters and chimneys and high slated roof. There had been another, a finer one, before this, we were told, standing in a different corner of the same park. A fine old gateway still remained with its heraldic carvings and mementoes of the past, but the road had travelled on elsewhere and no longer passed under it, as it did once long ago when the King's hunt used to come along the avenue which now led from nothing to nowhere. There is a description of this very place in Lucien Perey's delightful Memoirs of President Hénault and Madame Du Deffand.

"The first *château* belonged to the early days of Louis XV., and was inhabited by the great Maréchal de Villeroi," says the book. "Remy Hénault had a pretty country house at Etioles [Etioles comes back to me with its willow trees and dark amber canals]; it was the house that Madame de Pompadour afterwards lived in. Hénault used to spend part of the year there, and as his son was fond of sport he bought for him from the Maréchal de Villeroi a rangership and the place of Governor of Corbeil. The old Maréchal took a fancy to young Hénault and used to keep him to stay

at the *château* and also at his little house at
Soisy near Etioles. As ranger of the district
Hénault often received the Dauphin, the Duke
of Burgundy, and the Duke of Berry, who used
to come with a small suite to Villeneuve-Saint-
Georges. The Dauphin used to hunt wolves,
accompanied by the rangers ; the young princes
only shot pheasants. It is curious nowadays to
think of people hunting wolves at Villeneuve-
Saint-Georges," continues Lucien Perey, still
conjuring up my past, and then he gives a
note, saying : " The remains of the Château
de Villeroi still exist on the right hand of the
road from Corbeil to Mennecy, a road which is
always called in the country 'La route de
Villeroi.'" And this was the road along which
we used to straggle of summer evenings.

The people who were living at the *château*
when we lived at Mennecy (the first *château* I believe was burned down during the great Revolu-
tion) were retired manufacturers who had given
up business and who now dwelt at ease and in
dignity, sheltered by the high slated roofs and
chimneys of the old place. My grandparents
had been introduced to the family by our friend

the Maire, and when we all went up to call with
him one day, the younger members of the party
were not without hopes of finding some companions there, for we had seen a girl of about
our own age, who was, so the Maire told us, an
heiress and the only daughter of the house.
As we walked up through the park we met the
gardener, who left his work to escort us to the
front door, calling also to a maid who sat
darning stockings in the marble hall. She in
turn put down her work and disappeared
through a tall carved doorway, returning almost
immediately to ask us to go in. We found
ourselves in a big drawing-room with polished
floors, and with many tall windows opening to
the garden; some of them were shuttered and
curtained, and the room was rather dark. In it
sat, in a sort of semicircle of chairs ready
placed, the stout mother, the burly father, and
the broad-shouldered heiress in her plaid frock.
They received us very coldly, looking at us
aloof with curiosity and as if we had been
specimens of some strange unknown race. I
thought the gardener and the sewing-maid also
stared at us, when they returned, almost

immediately, with trays of refreshment,—biscuits and glasses of beer, which were handed round already poured out. I do not know if this was a custom peculiar to the neighbourhood, or only to this particular family. The young lady seemed surprised that we should refuse. "What, English, and you do not take beer?" she said, placing her tumbler between her knees. Between her draughts she then went on to ask us many questions about that strange country to which we belonged, about our out-landish ways and singular habits. It was a very different catechism from M. Malan's. "Did we ever go to church at all?" "Did we ever say any prayers?" "Did not heretics fast every Sunday instead of making it a fête-day?" "Had we ever heard of the Virgin Mary (surprise expressed) and the saints (more surprise)?" Our friend the Maire saw with pain that we young ladies were not getting on, and tried to bring the conversation round to other more congenial topics than those funda-mental differences for which we should all have burned one another a century before; he there-fore introduced the piano by way of a diversion,

the *charmant meuble* from Corbeil, and I could
see that we slightly rose in our host's estima-
tion, but I came away, all the same, very much
put out. It is disagreeable to be both damned
in the future and looked down upon in the
present, as one belonging to an ignorant and
barbarous race. I felt as if all the Catholic
saints in Paradise, certainly all the French ones,
were shrugging their shoulders at us when we
came away, and I spoke quite crossly to M. le
Maire when he asked me what I thought of the
château.

There used to be an odd stout figure walking about Mennecy in a workman's blouse and
loose trousers, and with a cropped head of black
hair and an old casquette. We were told that
it was a woman ; and a wholly supposititious
impression once arose in some one's mind that
it might have been George Sand herself. I
passed quite close on one occasion, when the
mysterious personage looked round and then
turned away, and I thrilled from head to foot.
How odd those mysterious moments are when
nothing seems to be happening, but which
nevertheless go on all the rest of one's life. I

saw a face stolid and sad, giving me an impression of pain and long endurance which
comes back still. It seemed to be a woman's
face, flabby and tanned, not old. There was
no gaiety in it, no adventure in the eyes; but
expiation, endurance, defiance, I know not what
tragedy was expressed by that thick-set down-
cast figure. I have now, alas, no doubt that it
was *not* George Sand. I had not read any of
her books then, but we had many things to
read in the old garden. There were various
books my father had given us and told us to
read during his absence, Macaulay's Essays
among them; and there was *Pendennis*, which
I had brought away from home, and which has
always seemed to me more like hearing him
talk than any other of his books; and above
all, there were his letters which came from time
to time. He was giving lectures at Manchester
and elsewhere before sailing for America, and
there is one of his letters folded in three and
addressed on the back to my sister at Mennecy,
Seine-et-Oise. "You see here is the stuck-up
hand as you like it best. . . . I have not a
great deal to say in the stuck-up hand. Ken-

sington is so gloomy that I can't stand it. . . .
How dismal it must be for poor Eliza [Eliza
was the housekeeper], who has no friends to
go to, who must stop in the kitchen all day.
As I think of her I feel inclined to go back and
sit in the kitchen with Eliza, but I dare say I
shouldn't amuse her much, and after she had
told me about the cat and how her father was,
we should have nothing more to say to one
another.   Last week I was away at Manchester,
when I broke down in a speech before 3000
ladies and gentlemen.   I felt very foolish, but
I tried again at night and did better, and as
there is nothing more wicked in breaking down
in a speech than in slipping on a bit of orange-
peel and breaking one's nose, why I got up
again, and made another speech at night without breaking down.   It's all custom, and most
people can no more do it than they can play
the piano without learning.   I hope you and
—— are learning hard to play me to sleep when
I come back from America.   I believe I am
going to Birmingham next week with the
lectures, and then to Manchester, and then,
——Steward, bring me a basin ! "

Many years afterwards, long after I married, the good and beautiful Lady Pease gave us the great pleasure of meeting Mr. John Bright at dinner at her house. I sat next Mr. Bright, and he began speaking to me of my father, and of this very time. "I remember," he said, "taking him to a meeting at Manchester, just before he went to America with his lectures. He broke down, and he was very much annoyed, and he said to me: 'Who will ever come and hear me lecture if I break down like this before such a number of people?' And I said to him: 'Never you mind; very few people don't break down at one time or another. You come along with me this evening; I'm going to another meeting; I'm not going to speak to fine fal-lal folks, but to a set of good, honest working men, and you must try again.' And he spoke," said Mr. Bright in his downright way, "and I never heard a better speech in all my life; it was a capital speech, and they were all delighted with him." And then and there Mr. Bright told me another little anecdote of my father, whom he had met a short while before his death at the Reform Club. He said that as he was

passing through the hall, he met him standing
in his way and he stepped back, took off his
hat, and stood with it in his outstretched hand.
"What is that for?" said Mr. Bright. "Why
do you hold your hat like that?" "Because I
see the most consistent politician I know going
by," said my father, "and I take off my hat to
him."

When my father sailed for America, people
were very kind to us, and wrote to us with
news of him. *Esmond* came for my grandmother, and a box which we received at Paris
puzzled us very much, and delighted us no less
than it puzzled us. It contained a magnificent
iced cake, anonymously and carefully packed
with strips of many-coloured paper. It was not
my father who had sent it, as we imagined, nor
was it till long afterwards that we discovered
that the sender was Mrs. Procter. Many
things are remembered of her; but how many
kind deeds there have been of hers without a
name to them!

Once the letters began to arrive from
America we were all much happier, for we
seemed in touch with him once more, and to

know what was happening. He was fairly
well and in good spirits, and making friends
and making money. I remember his writing
home on one occasion and asking us to send
him out a couple of new stomachs, so hospitable
were his friends over the water, so numerous
the dinners and suppers to which he was invited. When the long summer and winter
were over and the still longer spring, suddenly
one day we heard that he was coming back
much sooner than he expected. I believe
he saw a steamer starting for home and
could stand it no longer, and then and there
came off.

I can still remember sitting with my grandparents, expecting his return. My sister and I
sat on the red sofa in the little study, and
shortly before the time we had calculated that
he might arrive came a little ring at the front-
door bell. My grandmother broke down; my
sister and I rushed to the front-door, only
we were so afraid that it might not be he
that we did not dare to open it, and there
we stood until a second and much louder
ringing brought us to our senses. "Why

didn't you open the door?" said my father stepping in, looking well, broad, and upright, laughing.   In a moment he had never been away at all.

CHAPTER XI

TOUT CHEMIN——

AFTER his return from America my father took an apartment in Paris for the autumn months, and it was then that he told us he had made a plan for wintering in Rome. It almost seems to me now that all the rest of my life dates in some measure from those old Roman days, which were all the more vivid because my sister and I were still spectators and not yet actors in the play. I was just fifteen, my sister was still a little girl, but I thought myself a young woman. I have written elsewhere of Mrs. Kemble and Mrs. Sartoris and the Brownings, who were all living at Rome that winter, with a number of interesting people, all drinking, as we were about to do, of the waters of Trevi. How few of us returned to the fountain! But the proverb, I think, must apply to one's spiritual return. For, though one may drink and drink and go back again and again, it is ever a different person that stands by the fountain, whereas the shadowy self by the stone basin, bending over the rushing water, is the same, and does not change.

We started early in December, my father, my sister, and I. He had his servant with him, for already his health had begun to fail him. We reached Marseilles in bitter weather late one night. We laid our travelling plaids upon our beds to keep ourselves warm, but though we shivered, our spirits rose to wildest pitch next morning in the excitement of the golden moment. The wonderful sights in the streets are before me still—the Jews, Turks, dwellers in Mesopotamia, chattering in gorgeous colours and strange languages; the quays, the crowded shipping, the amethyst water. I can still see in a sort of mental picture a barge piled with great golden onions floating along one of the quays, guided by a lonely woman in blue rags with a coloured kerchief on her head. "There goes the Lady of Shalot," said my

father; and when we looked at him rather
puzzled, for we knew nothing of onions and
very little of Tennyson in those days, he
explained that a shalot was a species of onion,
and after a moment's reflection we took in his
little joke, feeling that nobody ever thought of
such droll things as he did. Then we reached
our hotel again, where there were Turks still
drinking coffee under striped awnings, and a
black man in a fez, and a lank British diplomat,
with a very worn face, who knew my father,
arriving from some outlandish place with piles
of luggage; and we caught sight of the master
of the hotel and his family gathered round a
soup tureen in a sort of glass conservatory, and
so went upstairs to rest and refresh ourselves
before our start that evening. All this
splendour and novelty and *lux mundi* had
turned our heads, for we forgot our warm
wraps and half our possessions at the hotel,
and did not discover, till long after the steamer
had started with all of us on board, how many
essentials we had left behind.

The sun was setting as we steamed out of
Marseilles, and the rocky Island of If stood

out dark and crisp against the rush of bright
wavelets; across which we strained our eyes to
see Monte Cristo in his sack splashing into the
water of the bay.   Then we got out to sea,
and the land disappeared by degrees.   How
the stars shone that night on board the big
ship !   The passengers were all on deck talking in a pleasant murmur of voices, broken by
laughs and exclamations.   Among them were
some people who specially attracted us, a very
striking and beautiful quartet from the north.
There was a lovely mother, oldish, widowed,
but very beautiful still; the two charming
daughters, one tall and lovely, the other a
piquant brunette; there was the son, one of
the handsomest young men I have ever seen.
They were going to Rome, they told us, for
the winter.   Christina, the eldest girl, was
dressed in white.   She seemed to me some fair
Urania, controlling the stars in their wondrous
maze as she and I and my sister paced the
deck till it was very late, and some bell
sounded, and my father came up and sent us
down to our cabin.   Then the night turned
bitter cold, and as we had left our shawls on

the shores of France, we made haste to get to
bed and to be warm. Though it was cold we
liked fresh air, and were glad to find that our
port-holes had been left open by the steward;
we scrambled into our berths, and fell asleep.
I lay at the top, and my sister in the berth
below. How well I remember waking suddenly in a slop of salt water! The ship was
sinking, we were all going to be drowned, and
with a wild shriek calling to my sister I sprang
from the cabin and rushed up the companion-
steps on deck. I thought she called me back,
but I paid no heed, as I reached the top of the
companion-ladder, dripping and almost in tears,
with my fatal announcement. There I encoun-
tered the steward, who began to laugh, and
who led me back crestfallen to our cabin, at
the door of which my sister was standing.
The water was dancing in, in a stream, and
the steward scolded us well as he screwed
up the port-holes and got us some dry bed-
ding. Next morning, to my inexpressible mor-
tification, I heard some people telling the
story. "She rushed on deck, and declared
the ship was sinking," said one voice to

another. I didn't wait to hear any more, but
fled.

The wind went down again, but it was still
bitter cold, and we shivered without our wraps,
as we steamed up to Genoa, along the
spreading quays with their background of
gorgeous palaces and cloud-capped towers.
There were convicts in their chains at work
upon the great steps of the quay, who stared at
us as we landed. And the very first thing
which happened to us when we found ourselves in
Italy at last—the land where citrons bloom,
where orange flowers scent the air—was that
we drove straight away to a narrow back street,
where we were told we should find a shop for
English goods, and then and there my father
bought us each a warm gray wrap, with stripes
of black, nothing in the least Italian or
romantic, but the best that we could get. And
then, as we had now a whole day to spend on
shore, and shawls to keep us warm, we drove
about the town, and after visiting a palace or
two took the railway, which had been quite
lately opened, to Pisa. The weather must have
changed as the day went on, for it was sun-

shine, not Shetland wool, that warmed us at
last ; but the wind was blowing still, and what
I specially remember in the open Piazza at
Pisa is the figure of a stately monk, whose
voluminous robes were fluttering and beating
as he passed us, wrapped in darkness, mystical,
majestic, with all the light beyond his stateliness
and the cathedral in its glory and the Leaning
Tower aslant in the sunlight for a background.

Our adventures for the day were not yet
over. At the station we found two more of the
ship's passengers, young men with whom we
had made acquaintance, and we all returned to
Genoa together. The train was late and we
had to be on board at a certain time, so that
we engaged a carriage and drove quickly to
the quay, where the convicts clanking in their
chains were still at work. A boat was found,
rowed by some sailors who certainly did not
wear chains, but who were otherwise not very
unlike those industrious convicts in appearance.
The bargain was made, we entered the boat all
five, and as we were getting in we could see our
great ship in the twilight looking bigger than
ever, and one rocket and then another going

off towards the dawning stars. "They are
signalling for us," said one of our companions :
"we shall soon be on board."

We had rowed some twenty strokes from the
shore by this time, when suddenly the boatmen
left off rowing, they put down their oars, and
one of them began talking volubly, though I
could not understand what he said. "What's
to be done ?" said one of the young men to my
father. "They say they won't go on unless we
give them fifty francs more," and he began
shaking his head and remonstrating in broken
Italian. The boatmen paid no attention,
shrugged their shoulders, and waited, as if they
were determined never to row another stroke.
Then the steamer sent up two more rockets,
which rose through the twilight, bidding us
hurry ; and then suddenly my father rose up in
the stern of the boat where he was sitting, and,
standing tall and erect and in an anger such as
I had never seen him in before or after in all
my life, he shouted out in loud and indignant
English, "D—n you, go on !" a simple male-
diction which carried more force than all the
Italian polysyllables and expostulations of our

companions. To our surprise and great relief, the men seemed frightened, and took to their oars again and began to row, grumbling and muttering. When we got on board the ship they told us it was a well-known trick the Genoese boatmen were in the habit of playing upon travellers, and that they would have sent a boat for us if we had delayed any longer.

We reached our journey's end next morning, and landed at Civita Vecchia about mid-day. This landing was no less wonderful than everything else, we thought, as we looked in awe at the glorious blaze of colour, at the square Campanile with its flat tiled roof, and at all that we were *going* to see, which was coming to meet us on the very shore. To begin with, there was the chorus from the Opera waiting in readiness, men with pointed hats and Italian legs, women in fancy dress, with fancy dress babies, all laughing, talking in Italian, and at home in Italy. We had some trouble in getting our luggage through the dogana. Most of the other travellers started before we did, and we were among the last to start for Rome. My father was anxious to get on, for there were

unpleasant rumours about brigands on the road.
Another family, Russians, with a courier, and a
great deal of luggage, was to follow us, and
some one suggested we should wait for their
escort; but on the whole my father decided to
start. The afternoon shadows were beginning
to lengthen, when at length we were packed
and ready. We had a mouldy post-chaise, with
a gray ragged lining, and our luggage on the
top. We hoped to get to Rome before dark.
I remember thrilling as my father buttoned his
overcoat and told us he had put his hundred
louis for safety into an inner pocket.

The country is not very beautiful between
Civita Vecchia and Rome—at least I do not
remember anything to distract our attention
from our alarms. We were just frightened
enough to be stimulated and amused as we
jolted past the wide fields where the men were
at work. We sat all three abreast in the jolting
old carriage: my father's servant was on the
box. We were reading our Tauchnitz books,
being tired of watching the flat horizons, when
suddenly the carriage stopped, and Charles
Pearman with a pale face of alarm came to the

window and said that one of the traces had
broken, and that there were a number of people
all coming round the carriage. We were
surrounded by people as if by magic—satyrs,
shepherds, strange bearded creatures with
conical hats, and with pitchforks in their hands.
The sun was just setting, and dazzling into our
faces all the time. For some five minutes we
waited, looking at each other in silence, and
wondering what was going to come next. At
the end of that time, and after a good deal of
conversation with the postilions, the satyrs and
fauns went their way with their pitchforks,
leaving us, to our inexpressible relief, to con-
tinue our journey. Then came the dusk at
last, and the road seemed longer and longer.
I think I had fallen asleep in my corner, when
my father put his hand on my shoulder.
"Look!" he said, and I looked, and, lo! there
rose the dusky dome of St. Peter's, gray upon
the dark-blue sky.

Very soon afterwards some one with a
lantern opened the gates of Rome, and
examined our passport, and let us in. We
drove to our hotel in the Via Condotti, and

when we awoke next morning it was to the sound of countless church bells in the morning light.

When we leant from the window of our entresol sitting-room, with its odd yellow walls, we could almost touch the heads of the passers-by. It was Sunday morning, all the bells were flinging and ringing: and they seemed to be striking and vibrating against that wonderful blue sky overhead. How well I remember my first Roman contadina, as she walked majestically along the street below; black-haired, white-becapped, white-besleeved, and covered with ornaments, on her way to mass.

The Piazza d'Espagna, at the end of our street, was one flood of sunshine, in which other contadinas and bambinos and romantic shepherds were floating when we came out to look and to wonder. Wonderful as it all was, it seemed also almost disappointing. We had expected, we didn't know what; and this was *something;* something tangible, and, so far less than we expected, appreciable. " Wait a little," said my father; "people are always a little disappointed when they first come to Rome."

I remember long after hearing Mr. Appleton say, " People expect to taste the result of two thousand years of civilisation in a morning: it takes more than a morning to receive so much into one's mind . . . a lifetime is not too long." Mr. Appleton was right when he said it takes a lifetime to realise some ideas. But now and then one certainly lives a lifetime almost in a comparatively flying minute; and those two months at Rome, short as they were, have lasted my lifetime. The people, the sights, the sounds, have never quite ceased for me yet. They have become an habitual association, and have helped to make that mental standard by which one habitually measures the events as they follow one another.

That first evening in Rome, as we sat at dinner at the table d'hôte, in the dark vaulted dining-room, all the people, I remember, were talking confusedly of an attack by brigands upon some Russians on the road from Civita Vecchia—the very vagueness of the rumour made it the more impressive to us.

There is a letter from my father to his mother which he must have written the very

next day : it is dated Hôtel Franz, Via Condotti,
December 6. "We have very comfortable
quarters at the hotel where I lived before," he
writes, "except for some animal that bit me
furiously when I was asleep yesterday on the
sofa. It can't be a bug, of course—the chamber-
maid declares she has never seen such a thing,
nor so much as a flea, so it must be a scorpion,
I suppose," and he goes on to compare St.
Peter's to Pisa. "We agreed Pisa is the best,"
he says. "The other is a huge heathen parade.
The founder of the religion utterly disappears
under the enormous pile of fiction and ceremony
that has been built round him. I'm not quite
sure that I think St. Peter's handsome. The
front is positively ugly, that is certain, but
nevertheless the city is glorious. We had a
famous walk on the Pincio, and the sun set for
us with a splendour quite imperial. I wasn't
sorry when the journey from Civita Vecchia
was over. Having eighty or ninety louis in my
pocket, I should have been good meat for the
brigands had they chosen to come."

Very soon our friends began to appear—
Mr. Browning, Mr. Sartoris, Mr. Æneas

Macbean. Mr. Macbean was the English
banker. He was the kindest of bankers, and
he used to send us great piles of the most
delightful books to read. Lockhart's, Scott's,
and Bulwer's heroes, and D'Israeli's saint-like
politicians all came to inhabit our palazzo when
we were established there. Zanoni and that
cat-like spirit of the threshold are as vivid to
me as any of the actual people who used to
come and see us, or our late fellow-travellers
(who now also seemed like old friends) as we
passed them, hurrying about in search of
lodgings. All that day we came and went; we
stood under the great dome of St. Peter's, we
saw the Tiber rushing under its bridges ; then
no doubt in consequence of the scorpions we
also went about to look for lodgings, and it was
Mr. Browning who told us where to go. One
can hardly imagine a more ideal spot for little
girls to live in than that to which he directed
us—to a great apartment just over the pastry-
cook's in the Palazzo Poniatowski, in the Via
Della Croce. We climbed a broad stone staircase with a handsome wrought-iron banister,
we clanged at an echoing bell, and a little old

lady in a camisole, rejoicing in the imposing name of Signora Ercole, opened the door, and showed us into a dark outer hall. Then she led the way from room to room, until we finally reached a drawing-room with seven windows, at which we exclaimed in preliminary admiration. Among the other items of our installation were a Chinese museum, a library, a dining-room with a brazen charcoal-burner in the centre, and besides all these we were to have a bedroom, a dressing-room, and a cupboard for my father's servant. My father took the dressing-room for himself. He put me and my sister into the big bedroom to the front, and the man retired to the cupboard in the hall. Signora Ercole, our landlady, also hospitably offered us the run of her own magnificent sitting-rooms, besides the four or five we had engaged. I have a vague impression of her family of daughters, also in camisoles, huddled away into some humbler apartment, but we saw little of them. We established ourselves comfortably in one corner of the great drawing-room, clearing an inlaid table of its lamps and statuettes, its wax flowers,

and other adornments.   Then we felt at home.
A stone-mason suspended at his work began to
sing in mid-air just outside one of the windows,
there came to us the sound of the pfifferari from
the piazza down below, and the flutter of the
white doves' wings and their flying shadows
upon the floor, together with a scent of flowers
and sense of fountains, and the fusty fascinating
smell from the old hangings and bric-à-brac.
I think the Ercoles must have done some
business in *brocanteurs*, for the furniture was
more like that of a museum than a human
living house : all over the walls they had rows
of paintings in magnificent gildings, of which
the frames were the most important parts.
All the same, the whole effect was imposing
and delightful, and we felt like enchanted
Princesses in a palace, and flew from room to
room.

About luncheon time my father sent us down
to the pastry-cook's shop, where we revelled
among cream tarts and *petits fours*, and then
we ordered our dinner, as people did then, from
a *trattoria* near at hand.   Then we went out
again, still in our raptures, and when dinner-

time came, just about sunset, excitement had given us good appetites, notwithstanding the tarts.

We were ready, but dinner delayed.

We waited more and more impatiently as the evening advanced, but still no dinner appeared. Then the English servant, Charles, was called, and despatched to the cook-shop to make inquiry. He came back much agitated, saying the dinner had been sent—that they assured him it had been sent! It had apparently vanished on its way up the old palace stairs. "Go back," said my father, "and tell them there is some mistake, and that we are very hungry, and waiting still." The man left the room, then returned again with a doubtful look. There *was* a sort of box came an hour ago, he said: "I have not opened it, sir." With a rush my sister and I flew into the hall, and there sure enough stood a square solid iron box with a hinged top. It certainly looked very unlike dinner, but we raised it with some faint hopes which were not disappointed! Inside, and smoking still upon the hot plates, was spread a meal like something in a fairy

tale—roast birds and dressed meat, a loaf of
brown bread and *compotes* of fruit, and a salad
and a bottle of wine, to which good fare we
immediately sat down in cheerful excitement—
our first Roman family meal together.

When people write of the past, those among
us who have reached a certain age are
sometimes apt to forget that it is because so
much of it still exists in our lives, that it is so
dear to us. And, as I have said before, there
is often a great deal more of the past in the
future than there was in the past itself at the
time. We go back to meet our old selves,
more tolerant, forgiving our own mistakes,
understanding it all better, appreciating its
simple joys and realities. There are compen-
sations for the loss of youth and fresh
impressions ; and one learns little by little that
a thing is not over because it is not happening
with noise and shape or outward sign : its roots
are in our hearts, and every now and then they
send forth a shoot which blossoms and bears
fruit still.

Early life is like a chapter out of Dickens,
I think—one *sees* people then : their tricks of

expression, their vivid sayings, and their quaint humours and oddities do not surprise one ; one accepts everything as a matter of course—no matter how unusual it may be. Later in life one grows more fastidious, more ambitious, more paradoxical; one begins to judge, or to make excuses, or to think about one's companions instead of merely staring at them. All these people we now saw for the first time, vivid but mysterious apparitions : we didn't know what they were feeling and thinking about, only we saw them, and very delightful they all were to look at.

Meanwhile our education was not neglected. We had a poetess to teach us a little Italian, a signora with a magnificent husband in plaid trousers, to whom I am sure she must have written many poems. Once she asked us to spend an evening in her apartment. It was high up in a house in a narrow street, bare and swept, and we found a company whose conversation (notwithstanding all Madame Eleonora Torti's instructions) was quite unintelligible to us. We all sat in a circle round the great brass brazier in the centre of the bare room. Every

now and then the host took up an iron bar
and stirred the caldron round, and the fumes
arose. Two or three of the elder people sat in
a corner playing cards—but here also we were
at fault. The cards represented baskets of
flowers, coins, nuts, unknown and mysterious
devices ; among which the familiar ace of
diamonds was the only sign we could recognise.

After these social evenings our servant used
to come to fetch us home, through moonlight
streets, past little shrines with burning lamps,
by fountains plashing in the darkness. We
used to reach our great staircase, hurry up half-
frightened of ghosts and echoes, and too much
alive ourselves to go quickly to sleep. Long
after my father had come home and shut his door
we would sit up with Mr. Macbean's heroes and
heroines, and read by the light of our flaring
candles till the bell of the Frate in the convent
close by began to toll.

CHAPTER XII

MRS. KEMBLE

My father was a very young man when he first knew the Kemble family. In 1832 he himself was twenty-one, a couple of years younger than Mrs. Fanny Kemble, who was born in 1809. The mentions of the Kemble family in a diary which he kept about that time are very constant. "Called at Kemble's. Walked with Kemble in the Park. [Kemble was John Mitchell Kemble, Mrs. Fanny Kemble's brother.] We met the Duke looking like an old hero," he writes. " Breakfasted with Kemble; went to see the rehearsal of the Easter piece at Covent Garden, with Farley in his glory." Again : "Called at Kemble's. He read me some very beautiful verses by Tennyson." On another occasion my father speaks of seeing " Miss Tot, a very nice girl. Madam not visible"; and again of "Miss Fanny still in Paris. . . ."

It was in the year 1851, or thereabouts, that my own scraps of recollections begin and that I remember walking with my father along the High Street at Southampton; and somewhere near the archway he turned, taking us with him into the old Assembly Rooms, where I heard for the first. and only time in all my life a Shakesperean Reading by Mrs. Fanny Kemble. I think it was the first time I ever saw her. She came in with a stiff and stately genuflexion to the audience, took her seat at the little table prepared for her, upon which she laid her open book, and immediately began to read. My sister and I sat on either side of our father. He followed every word with attention; I cannot even make sure of the play after all these years, but Falstaff was in it, and with a rout and a shout a jolly company burst in. Was it Falstaff and his companions, or were they

> Fairies, black, grey, green, and white,
> You moonshine revellers——?

Suddenly the lady's voice rose, with some generous cheery chord of glorious fun and jollity. I can hear the echo still, and see her action as she pointed outwards with both open hands, and my father with a start, bursting into sympathising laughter and plaudit, began crying "Brava! Brava!" and then again he sat listening and looking approvingly through his spectacles. As we came away he once more broke into praise. "Don't you see how admirably she forgets herself?" he said; "how she throws herself into it all? how finely she feels it?" My father was that best of audiences, a born critic and yet an enthusiast; and to the last he could throw himself into the passing mood, into the spirit of the moment, while at the same time he knew what it was he was admiring, and why he admired.

Some years passed before we met Mrs. Kemble again, in Rome. It was at a very hard and difficult hour of her life, so I have heard her say, a time when she needed all her courage to endure her daily portion of suffering. I was then a hobbledehoy, and (though she was no less kind to me then than in later years) I only stared and wondered at her ways, asking myself what she meant, and how much she meant by the things she said, for I only half understood her; but when I, too, was an older woman the scales fell from my eyes.

One had to learn something one's self before one could in the least appreciate her. When the gods touch one's hair with gray, then comes some compensating revelation of what has been and is still. Now I can understand the passionate way in which Mrs. Kemble used in early times to speak of slavery; then I used to wonder nor realise in the least what she felt, when she would sometimes start to her feet in agitation and passionate declamation; she who with streaming eyes and wrung heart had walked about the plantations feeling more, perhaps, than any slave could do what it was to be a slave. To her free and ruling nature every hour of bondage must have seemed nothing short of torture. In those far-back Roman days of which I have been writing, she used to take us out driving with her from time to time. "Where shall I drive to?" asks the coachman. "*Andate al Diavolo*," says Mrs. Kemble gaily. "Go where you will, only go!" And away we drive through streets, and out by garden walls and garden gates to the Campagna, and as we drive along she begins to sing to us. I could box my own past ears for wondering what the passers-by would think of it, instead of enjoying that bygone song.

I can also remember Mrs. Kemble sitting dressed in a black dress silently working all through the evening by her sister's fireside, and gravely stitching on and on, while all the brilliant company came and went, and the music came and went. In those days Mrs. Kemble had certain dresses which she wore in rotation whatever the occasion might be. If the black gown chanced to fall upon a gala day she wore it, if the pale silk gown fell upon a working day she wore it; and I can still hear an American girl exclaiming with dismay as the delicate folds of a white silk embroidered with flowers went sweeping over the anemones in the Pamphili Gardens. Another vivid impression I have is of an evening visit Mrs. Kemble paid Mrs. Browning in the quiet little room in the Bocca di Leone, only lit by a couple of tapers and by the faint glow of the fire. I looked from one to the other: Mrs. Browning welcoming her

guest, dim in her dusky gown unrelieved ; Mrs.
Kemble upright and magnificent, robed on this
occasion like some Roman empress in stately
crimson edged with gold.   It happened to be
the red dress day, and she wore it.   " How do
you suppose I could have lived my life," I once
heard her say, " if I had not lived by rule, if I
had not made laws for myself and kept to
them ? "   Out of this stress of feeling, out of
this passionate rebellion against fate, she grew
to the tender, the noble and spirited maturity
of her later days.   In time, by habit and
degrees, we learn to understand a little more
how to fit ourselves to circumstances, and life
begins to seem possible, and to contain certain
elements of peace and of philosophy ; it is in
mid-life, when we try to accommodate our own
wants and wishes to those of others, that the
strain is greatest and the problem occasionally
passes beyond our powers of solution.   Indeed
very few solutions are possible, though wise
compromises exist for us all.   Some are more
adaptable than others, and not having very
positive selves to manage, having impressions
rather than strong convictions to act upon, they

run fairly well along other people's lines; but when strong feeling, vivid realisations, passionate love of truth and justice, uncompromising faith exist, then experience becomes hard. indeed. When Mrs. Kemble went to her rest only the other day, the critics who spoke so inadequately of that great personality had not felt the influence of her generous inspiration. "A prouder nature never fronted the long humiliation of life," said Mr. Henry James who knew her, touching upon the more tragic side of her history.[1]

One should have a different language to speak with of each of those one has loved and admired in turn. Such a language exists in one's heart, but how can one translate it into print? Some people seem like green places in the desert; one thinks of them, and one is at rest. It is also true that there also exist a certain number who oppress one with nameless discouragement, bores past and present. But the Elect are those who put life into one, who give courage to the faint-hearted, hope, out of their

[1] In the *Atlantic Monthly* for May 1893, I also read a very remarkable and most interesting article about my old friend, by Mr. Lee, who had known her in her youth.

own hearts' constancy; to these Fanny Kemble belonged indeed. To the end she retained the power of making new friends, of being loved by them and of loving them. One member of my own family, whom the elder lady was pleased to christen Rosalind, only knew her when she was long past seventy years of age, but what a true and spontaneous friendship was that which sprang up between them both, one which added, so wrote Mrs. Wister, to the happiness of her mother's later years. Mrs. Kemble returned love with love in full measure, whether it came to her in the shape of beautiful white azaleas from an old friend's hand, or of music played so as to delight her fine taste, or even as *dumme Liebe* with nothing to say, nothing to show.

I once went out shopping with her one spring morning when she thought her room would look the brighter for muslin curtains to admit the light. She carried a long purse full of sovereigns in her hand. We drove to Regent Street to a shop where she told me her mother and her aunt used both to go. It may have been over that very counter that the classic

"Will it wash?" was uttered. The shopman, who had assuredly not served Mrs. Siddons, or he would have learned his lesson earlier in life, produced silken hangings and worsted and fabrics of various hues and textures, to Mrs. Kemble's great annoyance. I had gone to another counter and came back to find her surrounded by draperies, sitting on her chair and looking very serious; distant thunder seemed in the air. "Young man," she said to the shopman, "perhaps your time is of no value to you—to *me* my time is of great value. I shall thank you to show me the things I asked for instead of all these things for which I *did not* ask," and she flashed such a glance at him as must have surprised the youth. He looked perfectly scared, seemed to leap over the counter, and the muslin curtains appeared on the spot.

Mrs. Kemble once asked me suddenly what colour her eyes were, and confused and unready I answered, "Light eyes." At the moment indeed they looked like amber, not unlike the eyes of some of those captive birds one sees in their cages sitting alone in the midst of crowds. Mrs. Kemble laughed at my answer. "Light eyes! Where are your own? Do you not know that I have been celebrated for my dark eyes?" she said; and then I looked again and they were dark and brilliant, and looking at me with a half-amused half-reproachful earnestness.

It must have been in the early years of the century that Sir Thomas Lawrence sketched that well-known and most charming head of Miss Fanny Kemble with which we are most of us acquainted. The oval face, the dark eyes, the wise young brows, the glossy profusion of dark hair, represent her youth; she was no less striking in her age, though no great painter ever depicted it. She grew to be old indeed, but it was only for a little while that she *was* an old woman. Stately, upright, ruddy and brown of complexion, almost to the very last; mobile and expressive in feature, reproachful, mocking, and humorous, heroic, uplifted in turn. This was no old woman, feeling the throb of life with an intensity far beyond that of younger people, splendid in expression, vehement, and yet at times tender with a tenderness such as is very rare. She was

indeed one of those coming from the mountain, one of the bearers of good tidings. As a girl I used to watch Mrs. Kemble stitching at her worsted work, and so in later days we have all seen her, sitting stitching in her arm-chair, dressed in her black silk Paris dress and lace cap. She sits upright by the window, with flowers on the table beside her, while her birds are pecking in their cage. For a long time she kept and tended certain American mocking-birds, letting them out of their cages to fly about the room, and perch here and there upon the furniture. "I have no right," she used to say, "to inflict the annoyance of my pleasures upon my servants, and therefore I attend to my birds and their requirements myself." She emphasises her words as she sits at work, stitching in the long coloured threads with extra point as she speaks; or again, when she is interested in what she says, putting down her tapestry and looking straight into your face, as she explains her meaning directly and clearly, without fear of being misunderstood. I once complained to her of something said by some one else. "I do not care what any one thinks of me, or chooses to say of me "—I can almost hear her speak—" nay, more than that, I do not care what any one chooses to say of the people I love ; it does not in any way affect the truth. People are at liberty to speak what they choose, and I am also at liberty not to care one farthing for what they say, nor for any mistakes that they make." What Mrs. Kemble did care for, scrupulously, with infinite solicitude, was the fear of having ever caused pain by anything that she had said in the energy of the moment ; she would remember it and think over it after days had passed. People did not always understand her, nor how her love of the truth, as it appeared to her, did not prevent her tenderness for the individual ; she would also take it for granted, that whoever it was she was talking to also preferred the truth to any adaptation of it. Her stories of the past were endlessly interesting and various. She had known everybody interesting as well as uninteresting. She had always detested banalities, and even as a girl she seems to have had the gift of making other people speak out of their hearts. Her pathetic story of Mary Shelley haunts one with the saddest persistence, and seems to sigh back the curtain of the past. " Bring up a boy to think for himself," she as a girl once said to Mrs. Shelley; and to this came the mother's passionate answer, "Ah! no, no, bring him up to think like other people."

Mr. Henry James instances among her other social gifts, her extraordinary power of calling up the representation of that which was in her mind, and impressing others with her own impression. Those, he says, who sometimes went with her to the play in the last years of her life, will remember the Juliets, the Beatrices, the Rosalinds, whom she could still make vivid without any accessory except the surrounding London uproar.

I myself fortunately once happened to ask her some question concerning *As You Like It*, which had been Mrs. Sartoris's favourite play. Suddenly, as if by a miracle, the little room seemed transformed; there were the actors, no, not even actors; there stood Rosalind and Celia themselves, there stood the Duke, there was Orlando in the life and spirit. One spoke and then another, Rosalind pleading, the stern Duke unrelenting; then somehow we were carried to the Forest with its depths and its delightful company. It all lasted but a few moments, and there was Mrs. Kemble again sitting in her chair in her usual corner; and yet I cannot to this day realise that the whole beautiful mirage did not sweep through the little room, with colour and light and emotion, and the rustling of trees, and the glittering of embroidered draperies.

Mrs. Kemble told me that she herself had only once heard her aunt, Mrs. Siddons, read. She said the impression was very overpowering, though she had been almost a child at the time. It was from the witches' scene in *Macbeth* that Mrs. Siddons read. She was very old and broken at the time, and living in retirement, but for a moment she forgot her suffering state. The sense of storm and mystery and power was all round about, Mrs. Kemble said. One can imagine the scene, the dark-eyed maiden sitting at the feet of the great actress and receiving initiation from her failing hands.

The true dramatic faculty does not indeed depend on footlights, or on a stage; it is a

special gift from spirit to spirit. Fanny
Kemble was almost the very last representative
of the ruling race to which she belonged, and
in no small degree did she retain to the very
end their noble gift of illumination, of giving
life to words and feelings. She herself has
defined this power. " Things dramatic and
things theatrical are often confounded together,"
she writes. " English people, being for the
most part neither one nor the other, speak as if
they were identical, instead of so dissimilar
that they are nearly opposite. That which is
dramatic in human nature is the passionate,
emotional, humorous element, the simplest
portion of our composition ; that which imitates
it is its theatrical reproduction. The dramatic
is the real of which the theatrical is the false.
A combination of the power," she continues,
" of representing passion and emotion with that
of imagining or conceiving it, is essential to
make a good actor ; their combination in the
highest degree alone makes a great one."

I remember Mrs. Sartoris once saying, " I
do not know if you will think it very conceited
of me ; but it always seems to me that no one

I ever talk to seems able to say anything clearly and to the point, except myself and my sister Fanny. When she speaks, I know exactly what she means and wants to say; when other people speak, I have to find out what they mean, and even then I am not certain that they know it themselves." As Mrs. Sartoris spoke, she looked at me with her searching glance; her beautiful head was like that of some classical statue nobly set upon her shoulders. But no classical statue ever looked at you as she did; her eyes and mouth spoke before she uttered. She always seemed to me an improvisatrice. Both these women had the rare power of stirring and stimulating one's sleepy makeshift soul, suggesting, satisfying. It was as if Mrs. Sartoris could at will compel the sound and the sense and the colour into that in which she was interested, she created as she spoke instead of only speaking, so that we were all for the time, and indeed for a lifetime since, illumined by her.

Mrs. Sartoris was living in Paris in the Rue Royale, at one time, in a very stately apartment. It seemed to suit her, as did all handsome and

P

beautiful things.   I do not suppose the modern
æsthetic taste would have suited her.   She
liked glorious things full of colour, Italian,
sumptuous, and she liked them used for daily
life and pleasure.   She made a home out of
her lovely bric-à-brac and tapestries ' and
cabinets.   Something of course must be allowed
for the grateful excitement of inexperience, but
to us in those days, her houses seemed like
succeeding paradises upon earth.   I can
remember on one occasion gazing in admiration
at a glowing shaded lamp, the first I had ever
seen, reflected from one glass to another, and
listening to my hostess as she sang Oberon's
" Mermaid Song," from the far end of the room.
Then came dinner in an octagon dining-room
at a round table with pink wax candles and ices,
and then a quick drive to the theatre where our
stalls were kept for us.   I remember neither
the name of the theatre nor of the play, only the
look of the bright lighted stage, and the pretty
white house full of spectators.   Mrs. Sartoris
was using a pair of turquoise eye-glasses, through
which she looked about, and presently she whis-
pered to me, " There, to your left in the box on

the first tier." I looked expecting I know not
what, and my first impression was disappointment. I saw some figures in the box, two men
standing at the back, and a lady in a front seat
sitting alone. She was a stout middle-aged
woman, dressed in a stiff watered-silk dress,
with a huge cameo, such as people then wore,
at her throat. Her black shiny hair shone like
polished ebony, she had a heavy red face,
marked brows, great dark eyes; there was
something—how shall I say it?—rather fierce,
defiant, and set in her appearance, powerful,
sulky; she frightened one a little. "That is
George Sand," said Mrs. Sartoris, bending her
head and making a friendly sign to the lady
with her eye-glasses. The figure also bent its
head, but I don't remember any smile or change
of that fixed expression. The contrast struck
me the more, for my hostess, as I have said,
scarcely needed to speak to make herself
understood; her whole countenance spoke for
her even if she was silent. George Sand
looked half-bored, half-far-away; she neither
lighted up nor awoke into greeting.[1]

[1] I like better to think of George Sand as I never saw her, with

Mrs. Kemble once said she had heard George Sand described half in fun as "unamiable, very emphatic, very dictatorial, very like herself, in short"; but perhaps the description was as superficial in one case as it assuredly would have been in the other.

Mrs. Kemble was dramatic rather than dictatorial. Her selection of facts was curiously partial and even biassed; not so her uncompromising sense of their moral value. When she sat with her watch open before her, reading, writing, working to rule, it was because time itself was of importance in her eyes, rather than her work. For her, life belonged to time, rather than time to life. "Do you think I could have borne with my life if I had not lived by rule?" she used to say. She carried her love of method into everything, even into the game of Patience with which she amused herself. Evening after evening the table would be set

gray hairs and a softened life, outcoming and helpful and living in later years among her plants, and her grandchildren, and her poor people; to imagine her as I have heard her described in her age, beneficent, occupied, tending and prescribing, distributing the simples out of her garden, healing the sick, softened by time, giving to others day by day what she still earned by her nights of persistent work.

and the appointed number of games would be
played conscientiously, as she sat, whether she
was tired or not, inclined or not, as a beloved
enchantress dealing out passing destinies to the
pasteboard men and women on the table before
her. Mrs. Kemble once sent over for a
neighbour to teach him Patience; one might
moralise over the combination,—Mrs. Kemble
teaching Patience in her grand-seigneur fashion
and meekly subservient to its laws! It was
indeed because she was so conscious of
passionate interests and diversities, that she
tried to shape her life to one recurring pattern.
A friend recalls an ancedote of Frederika
Bremer, who was not willing to see Mrs. Kemble
on one occasion, explaining afterwards, " I could
not see so many people as you are when I had
a headache." She was indeed many people,
actors and musicians, philosophers, teachers,
and poets, in one. She was eighty before she
attempted a novel, but her letters are models,
especially the earlier ones. Her poems are
very lovely. Her Farewell to the Alps was
written after threescore years and ten had
passed over her head, and I heard her read it

with tears. Once I asked her why she so disliked the stage, loving all that belonged to it as she did. She said that it was because she loved her own being even more than her art; that she found the constant simulation of emotion in time destroyed in herself the possibility of natural feeling, and that she wished to keep the possession of her own soul; but I think she has also written this somewhere in her *Records*.

Perhaps the most distinguishing stamp of her character was her great and fervent piety. Her convictions were very deep; what she said of her own religious faith was that it was "invincible, unreasoning." I have heard a friend describe how, as they came along the mountain pass from Roselaui, Mrs. Kemble made her bearers set her down at the summit of the ascent. "I will lift up mine eyes unto the hills," she said, breaking out into the words of the Psalm, and repeating verse after verse. She used to go regularly to church when she was in London, though I do not think any of the steeples and pulpits which adorn South Kensington exactly suited the deep and fervent spirit of her faith. She was neither High Church nor Low Church nor Broad Church, and once after witnessing a Catholic ceremony, *Fête Dieu*, in some foreign city, she exclaimed to her foreign man-servant, " Oh, Govert, what an amusing religion you have! " But her faith was a noble one, and her great reverence for what was good and great seemed to make goodness and greatness nearer to us.

Of all possessions, that of the added power which comes to us through the gifts of others is one of the most mysterious and most precious. We are inadequate in a thousand ways, but the grace is there.

Mrs. Kemble possessed to a rare degree the gift of ennobling that to which she turned her mind.   Kindness is comparatively commonplace, but that touch which makes others feel akin to qualities greater than any they are conscious of in themselves, was, I think, the virtue by which she brought us all into subjection.

Printed by R. & R. CLARK, *Edinburgh.*

Printed in the United Kingdom
by Lightning Source UK Ltd.
123484UK00002B/81/A